SO-AZV-408

Promises & Epiphanies:
Life Revelations Through Poetry and Prose

SHERYL LEIGH ROBERTSON

Copyright © 2014 Sheryl Leigh Robertson

All rights reserved.

ISBN-13: 978-0615977744
ISBN-10: 06159774X

To the woman I am becoming,
And to those who have
Inspired, encouraged, supported,
And loved me
Along the way.

CONTENTS

Note: Italics denote titles of poems

"There are years that ask questions and years that answer."
~ *Zora Neale Hurston*

Promises and Epiphanies

The night sky absent a single star to wish upon,
I chose instead
To cast my cares on You.
And no matter what I asked of Thee,
Each time You responded
With either promise or epiphany.

At midnight—
With a dark, empty sky overhead,
Desolation lying ahead,
I could feel You there
Promising endless possibilities;
Comforting me with the epiphany
That any and every living thing
Emerged from a vast expanse of nothing;
Reminding me that Your work has always begun at night;
Promising that darkness is a prelude to light.

In the wee morning hours—
While quiet crept eerily 'round the earth
And I dared not make a sound,
You assured me that
Silence was better than discord
And promised that one day beautiful notes
Would blend into perfect chords.
Reflecting on the words You uttered in the beginning,
I had an epiphany
That life's simplest melodies
Can be enhanced with the harmony
Of three powerful words:
"Let there be…"

Awaiting dawn—
Finding no star to cast my hopes upon,
I wish, instead, on Thee;
Holding tight to Your promises,
Replaying my epiphanies.

Introduction

We spend our lives searching, be it for meaning, for love, for happiness, for acceptance, for answers to our incessant questions.

The lucky ones find these golden treasures quickly and with ease. Most of us, however, struggle. We scour the landscape of our lives and then dig down deep into the depths of our souls, desperately trying to find those things which elude us.

We all search in different ways. An important part of my quest has occurred in written form. When my questions, doubts, and fears have sought a safe place to express themselves without threat of judgment, they have always found a haven in my writings. Each piece I penned was a prayer uttered subconsciously, and in baring my soul through words, I have slowly uncovered answers, reassurances, and courage.

Promises & Epiphanies chronicles a life dedicated to the search. On my journey to self-discovery and understanding, I made pit stops to write poetry and prose when exhaustion threatened to overtake me. As the emotions poured from my soul in impassioned stanzas and inquisitive paragraphs, God spoke peace to my anxious mind. He gave me promises and epiphanies that encouraged me to keep moving forward.

I have taken some of the most important pieces from my journey—a representation of not only my thoughts and emotions but also of God's promises and epiphanies—and scattered them throughout these pages. This is a compilation of poems; spoken word pieces; personal essays; and posts from my blog, *Sheryl's Pearls*. Each was written to stand alone, and some were written for the ear rather than the eye, but together, they form an anthem for myself and others who have found the search to be a struggle.

The book is arranged into four sections: Dusk, Midnight, Daybreak, and Morning. Follow me through a season of darkness and confusion to arrive with me at a point of light and realization. Walk with me through my hodgepodge of questions and feelings on key moments related to love, dreams, faith, and happiness—because that is exactly what life is: a jumble of events, thoughts, and emotions in seemingly random order that ultimately, in hindsight, make sense.

Because the quest for understanding is universal and unending, I believe that you will see aspects of yourself in these pages and parts of your journey in its pieces. I pray that the book will help you to discover God's promises for your own life and to embrace the startling simplicity of your God-given epiphanies.

Dusk

Dusk

The sun is setting,
Dulling my radiant world.
My joy is clouded
By defeat and uncertainty.
As night falls,
People rush to cozy homes
Filled with laughter and love.
Finding my own land fallow,
My smile is fading
As rapidly as the light.
Once recognizable surroundings
Now seem foreign.
I search for a familiar
Glimpse of You.
Holding true to Your promise
Never to leave,
You appear
In a sliver of moonlight.
You are a beacon of hope.

A Blues for Summer

I awoke this morning missing you. Missing you the way one misses a departing lover whom one still has the pleasure of lying next to—replaying yesterdays and stalling tomorrows.

Our relationship is a simple one. Each day, your sunbeams kiss my face good morning and your warm temperatures drape themselves across my bare shoulders. In turn, I flirtatiously hike up the hemline on my dresses and let your evening breezes play in my hair. Our love is easy, complementary, comfortable.

Yet I can feel you pulling away. Your passion is less intense, the warmth slowly fading from your touch. Your moods are becoming less predictable, your usual sunny disposition spotted with occasional cold fronts. Some days, you are altogether absent. You return a day or two later, beaming like nothing happened. I melt in the warmth of your embrace, pushing away the nagging feeling that you are destined to leave again.

Like anyone who recognizes the beginning of the end, I am considering the role I played. I should have criticized less. Hugged you tightly even when I felt ugly, hot, and sticky. Wiped my brow during our hard times without sigh or complaint.

I should have cherished you. Sat at rooftop bars sipping daiquiris and mojitos. Sprawled out in parks across faded old blankets, soaking up the warmth of your touch. Strolled in silence during long walks by the water. I should have lingered in your presence.

Realizing that we now have more days behind us than ahead, I am making plans to do all the things I have been putting off for tomorrow. Making my way to the beach to lie lazily next to you. Finding occasions to wear cute dresses I purchased with you in mind. Taking late-night drives to nowhere, the wind whipping through my hair. Staring dreamily at starry night skies. Loving you "quickly, like the time is running out on us."[1] Because it is.

You will leave soon. I have picked up your dropped hints that this was never meant as forever.

Our relationship will end as flings do: without fanfare. To spare us the awkward goodbye, you will steal away in the quiet of night as I lay sleeping. I will wake to find your belongings gone, a few photographs and my memories serving as the only proof that you ever came at all.

I will not attempt to make you stay. Somehow, I can sense that my love would be less intense, less sincere if I had you with me always. What we had was characterized by longing and the satisfaction of attainment; then the desperation to stretch out the moments; followed by an inevitable, painful goodbye. It is this, the cycle of our love, that makes us beautiful.

While you are away, I will continue with life and make other friends. I'll flirt with Fall and snuggle up to Winter, even have a fling with Spring. What else is a girl to do?

But you will always have my heart. When you return, I'll be right here where you left me, ready to begin again with you.

Exodus

"It's getting late," you say.
"I should go
Before I overstay my welcome."
Even though
In that place beyond reason and reproach,
We both know
You were always wanted.
A bright vacancy sign hung from my heart
When you found me.
So I cannot blame you for making use of my revolving door.
I took a page from Lady Liberty,
Proclaiming:
"Give me your tired, your poor,
Your huddled masses yearning to breathe free,"
But never stopped to ask
Whether I could afford
The expense.
Now I stand on these shores
That I have called home
For a lifetime,
Which you have only dared to roam
For a moment,
And watch
Your exodus.

When the Heart Speaks

When the heart speaks, she sounds the alarm.

She has been there all along. Every moment of every day. Beating, pumping, contracting, expanding. In silence.

But when she speaks, she sounds the alarm.

We fail to notice her presence on the lackluster occasions that account for the overwhelming majority of our existence. Days, weeks, months pass with her quietly doing her do. Expand. Contract. Expand. Contract. We are none the wiser.

We fail to hear her over the muddled thoughts in our heads and the raucous soundtrack of the outside world. We cannot see her through the shield of body armor protecting her virtue. Distracted by the impetuous sensations that touch us day in and day out, we cannot feel her either.

But when she speaks, she sounds the alarm.

This silent, beautiful vessel makes her presence known when our souls are either brimming with love or crouched over in agony. In times of bliss, vulnerability, betrayal, joy, and offense, she asserts herself. It is then that she beats wildly, tired of being ignored and refusing to be forgotten.

In these moments of extraordinary highs and lows, she quickens her beat, resorting to urgent palpitations. She pulses with intensity. She squeezes a little harder than necessary, holds on a few seconds too long. She wraps her arms around herself and presses tightly, wringing out her insides like they are the Saturday morning wash. Elation, frustration, joy, and sorrow drip into the puddle of your soul.

"Just wanted to remind you I was here," she says. "Just wanted to mark this moment of exquisite enchantment. Just wanted to accentuate this disappointment with some piercing pain.

"Just wanted you to feel alive."

A Love Story

On a cold, bare hardwood floor,
Limbs curled up in the fetal position.
Flesh bruised, aching, and sore,
Exhausted from the inquisition.
Faith shaken to the core
And scared *this* beating will send her to the mortician—
There, a woman finds love.

On stark white sheets atop a hard bed,
Shivering from the finality of the deed.
Ears ringing with the cries of the premature dead,
Womb raw and mind reeling at full speed,
Weak from the tears and blood she's shed,
Desperate and unsure how to proceed—
There, a girl finds love.

In a scalding bath, inhaling a candle's vanilla scent,
Solo on what should have been her wedding day.
Guzzling wine in a sea of bubbles and torment,
Remembering how *she* had begged *him* to stay.
Now ashamed that she would have been content
To allow him to stray and betray
Just for the sake of having him present—
There, a woman finds love.

In these different yet similar situations—
When a lover's hands left one black and blue,
When guilt and fear led another to end God's creation,
And when abandonment left the other with no one to cling to,
Each of these women had her own personal revelation.
Because sometimes,
Under the influence of loneliness and desperation,
You will manage to do
The very thing you swore you would never do.
And for the things you vowed not to accept,
You'll become the model of acclimation,
Breaking your promise not to settle for love that isn't true.

And there you'll stand,
Stranded at the crossroads of devastation and isolation,
Feeling a hurt so intense
That neither drugs nor drinks can numb or bring you through.
Having looked for love in all the wrong places,
At last you'll tire of the exploitation.
And then, when you're completely alone,
Without a single person to turn to,
You will come to the realization
That you need God
And that He loves you.

Like them,
In Him, I found love.
And it's deeper than any that I've felt before,
Sweeter than those Luther sang of,
Greater than those Hollywood made me long for.

And as this sweet relationship unfolds,
I don't worry if it's too soon to call or when I'll see Him again.
I only say His name and He appears
Faithfully, regardless of where or when,
Ready and willing to lend an attentive ear.
Even when I'm long-winded, He listens in suspense,
Interested in every matter, great or small.
I can speak my mind without worrying He'll take offense,
And He knows me so well I don't have to say anything at all—
We're so close we're comfortable in the silence.
And I can confess my wrongs to Him without the threat
That He will later throw them back in my face.
He is the only one who can both forgive *and* forget,
For He is the originator of mercy and grace.
And He's not the least bit insecure
Or concerned about those who came before
Because He knows the reasons why we split,
And that human nature will not permit
Them to give me the type of love my soul longs for.

I, like those women who found love
At the beginning of this piece,
Have quit looking for Prince Charming
And have fallen into the arms of the Prince of Peace.

I'm complete and content with the King of kings.
All pining for a knight in shining armor has ceased.
God comes to my rescue with perfect timing.
Call me Sleeping Beauty,
For He awakened my soul when I was nearly deceased.
And that is why I love Him—
Because when nothing else could help,
His love lifted me.[2]
And He loved me not just in one moment
Or for a brief season;
His love endures forever.
He is the source of my joy,
My very reason
For living altogether.

I vow to love the Lord with all my heart and soul;
No one else can even compare.
So if you're broken like those women
And want to be made whole,
If you're down and don't want to stay there,
If you're a few moments shy of the world taking its toll,
One load short of all that you can bear,
Look to the Lord
With Heaven as your goal.
You'll find love and solace there.

Duality

Have you ever fallen victim to dueling emotions? Just plopped right down in your feelings and let them push you on their mood swings?

Have you ever felt uncomfortable in your own skin—like it was crawling with suppressed thoughts and emotions determined to gnaw their way out? Ever marvel at the unique creation that is you—so impressed with the intricate pieces fitting perfectly together that you wanted to pinch that same formerly crawling skin to see if you were real?

Have you ever felt painfully insignificant—and then spectacularly brilliant?

Have you ever found some part of you—either visible to the naked eye or concealed in the heart—so repulsive that you hid from bathroom mirrors and the people whose presence was a reflection of your shame? Ever had someone declare an ugly part of you breathtakingly beautiful and, for a moment, believed them? Ever had a day in which every part of you conspired to make you absolutely gorgeous?

Have you ever been so giddy that you couldn't frown if you wanted to, the edges of your mouth permanently Heaven bound? Have you ever walked through life on auto-smile, your facial muscles forming fraudulent grins on cue? Ever gotten so good that you fooled yourself?

Have you ever wanted to be everywhere and nowhere at the same time?

Have you ever longed for the days of Miss Mary Mack hand games and ice cream cones that left a sticky residue on your lips yet never stuck to your hips? Ever played host to a moment so perfect you wanted to freeze time and then replay it over and over into your forever? Have you ever experienced an occasion so wrong that you wished you could race past it into whatever future would silence the involuntary wail escaping your throat?

Have you ever wanted something with every fiber of your being—then had your heart ache with longing for the opposite? Have you wondered if getting one would make you hate it out of loyalty to the other?

Have you ever been so sure of something that you would bet your life on it? Ever awoken the next day in a fog of uncertainty, your mind grappling to make sense of everything but your name?

Have you ever thought failure was impossible—then after thinking that endeavor over once more, decided success was improbable?

Have you ever felt your foot tapping impatiently on your life's floor, beckoning that next great moment? Ever had a change of heart and wished you could buy yourself some time before the greatness made its grand entrance?

Have you ever wondered where all this was going? Have you ever been afraid to get to "the end?"

I guess that's where faith comes in.

I guess that's what keeps life interesting.

I guess I was just wondering.

Conversations with Me

I have this good friend,
And we have some of the most profound conversations.
No topic is off limits;
She knows my dreams and aspirations,
Bears my burdens and frustrations.
Closer to me than any person on earth,
She's always there, regardless the situation.
But there's just one thing—
Sometimes she can undergo the most drastic transformation.
From best friend to worst enemy,
Source of motivation to queen of intimidation.
Loudest cheerleader to biggest skeptic,
She fuels my confidence and my reservations.
She hurls insults with the aim of an MLB pitcher,
Blatantly misusing insider information.
But she can't really talk because she's guilty by association.
She's also guilty of character assassination,
Slandering my reputation and making unfounded accusations.
She has an annoying fixation on all that I'm not
And a perplexing preoccupation with the past.
I often question this friend's dedication
And ponder whether she and the devil are in collaboration
To destroy me.
I love, but sometimes truly dislike, this friend.
Yet I cannot be rid of her—
For I am she.

On a pretty good day,
My conversations with me begin bright and early
As I stand before the mirror and pick apart
The image staring back at me.
I trace the blemishes, question the alignment of my teeth,
And attempt to pinch away my larger-than-life cheeks.
I pounce on imperfections and downplay assets,
Even fret over future flaws that have not appeared yet.
I criticize the wide hips and thick legs passed down my family tree.
I thought I had finally accepted I would never look like the chicks on TV.
But despite yesterday's breakthrough,
Today, it's bothering me.
      Then I hear a whisper:
You are fearfully and wonderfully made in the image of Me.

On an average day,
My focus shifts from my outer being to the soul inside.
I'm confused and feel as if I'm wandering through life with no true guide.
Should I go east, west, north, south—I just can't decide.
I'm praying for a single sign that God has not cast me aside.
I'm losing sight of dreams deferred and discouraged by wishes denied.
Wondering when I'll get that dream job,
Or if I'll ever become a bride.
Sometimes I don't know what to pray for
And other times I find myself succumbing to pride,
Refusing to repeat that same request one more time,
Hoping God gets that some things are just implied.
   Then I remember:
Just as His eyes are on the little sparrow,[3]
With me does He also abide.
There's no need to question or fear,
For every need will be supplied.
Though I'm inadequate by myself,
What I lack, He will provide.

On a bad day,
I'm before the mirror again,
But my previous wrongs make it hard to meet my own eyes.
My mind chastises: "Remember when—? What about the time—?"
As it replays a track of former sins and lies.
And if the past is any indication of the future, it implies
Days of hurt, shame, and lows so low they overshadow my highs.
If only I could climb back into my mother's womb,
Kiss this world goodbye,
Then arise anew—jubilant, confident, and wise.
   But I know
I must live in the present, strive for a better future;
The past I can't revise.
I wonder, will I always be a slave to guilt?
My soul replies:
I know I've been changed, and His mercies are new with every sunrise.

On an awful day,
My soul, like the apostle Paul's, is afflicted with faction.
I desire to do good, but can't quite put it into action.
And to the evil I do not want to do, I have this innate attraction.
I'm struggling to resist temptation and ignore distraction,
Fearful that one slip-up will result in a chain reaction.

Then I'm reminded:
What I'm experiencing is not even a fraction of what He endured,
And I've been rescued from this body of death by Christ's compassion. [4]

I don't need anyone to tell me how horrible I am or what I'll never be.
I hear it repeatedly in my conversations with me—
Conversations fighting to claim my sanity.
Bad days to good days,
Rising one moment, the next I'm sinking.
It's been so bad I've prayed I would just stop thinking.
But that's a prayer God seems to always deny.
Instead He joins my conversations and tells me how to survive.
Yes, I will have good days and bad days and all kinds in between.
But thank God for the Resurrection Day, which has washed my soul clean;
A day that reminds me of the power of love and gives me reason to hope,
That assures me my future is bright
And there's nothing with which I can't cope.

So on those pretty good days
As I begin to count my physical shortcomings,
I can now see my beauty through the eyes of my Creator.
He whispers words to make me smile a little wider,
Hold my head a little higher, and walk a little straighter.
On those average days
When I wonder which direction to turn and what lies ahead,
God reminds me that He's numbered each hair on my head.
"For I know the plans I have for you," He said.
"Plans to prosper you and not to harm you,
To give you a future and a hope."[5]
Regardless the situation,
How steep or slippery the slope,
Everything, even tests and trials that may not be understood,
Are all working together for my good.[6]
On those bad days
When I'm filled with shame and regret,
God tells me that my sins have been cast
As far as the east is from the west.[7]
It was finished when Jesus paid the ultimate price on Calvary;[8]
Now I just have to work on forgiving me.
And on those awful days
When I worry about sins that I have not even attempted,
God tells me that Christ can help me
Because He himself suffered when He was tempted.[9]

Thank God that in all my conversations with myself,
There is always a third party listening in.
He silences that negative, nagging voice within
And replaces it with His own.
He tells me that because He sits on the throne
With all power,
I need not fear the unknown.
He helps me to realize
That Satan attacks with fear and self-loathing
That only seek to rob me of God's blessings.
He tells me there's no need for guessing and stressing.
He encourages me to keep pressing
Toward the mark for the prize of the high calling.[10]
He tells me that my refusal to try
Is the only thing He'd find appalling.
His voice grows increasingly louder
In each and every conversation with me,
Setting my mind, body, and soul completely free
And slowly teaching me
How to truly love me.

Confronting the Unknown

I had been postponing a trip to the doctor for weeks. While I was sure I did not have a serious illness, something was not right. Still, I put it off.

Finally, as the weeks turned to months and the problem persisted, I gave in and scheduled an appointment. As I considered the absurdity of my unwillingness to confront the issue, I realized that we often treat God the same way I treated my doctor: we avoid Him.

Oddly enough, I put my health insurance to good use on a very regular basis. I typically run to the doctor as soon as I notice something is amiss. What was different about this situation? The issue was not life-threatening, but I was stalling on a doctor's visit because I knew it was indicative of a larger problem that I was not prepared to address.

I knew this larger problem existed. It crossed my mind often, but I did not want to add it to the full plate that was my life. I also knew my doctor. She would make me talk about it. She would connect the dots between the little issue and my bigger predicament. She would want to discuss other aspects of my life that were contributing factors. Talking about this small issue would only be a warm-up to the main event: a discussion about *me*.

If we are honest with ourselves, we have to admit there are little problems in our lives that we don't bring to God because we suspect they are evidence of larger issues that we would rather not handle. We know that God is like my doctor, determined to talk about what is *really* wrong with you. He does not treat symptoms but addresses the root of the problem. Therefore, after you have consulted Him, He will expect you to take action.

In Psalm 139, David says: "You have searched me, Lord, and you know me. You know when I sit and when I rise; you perceive my thoughts from afar. You discern my going out and my lying down; you are familiar with all my ways." *(Verses 1-3, New International Version [NIV])*

God has searched us. He knows us intimately. He sees the parts of us that we attempt to hide from ourselves.

David continues, "Where can I go from your Spirit? Where can I flee from your presence? If I go up to the heavens, you are there; if I make my bed in the depths, you are there." *(Verses 7-8)*

There is no escaping God. He is walking with you daily, with a front row view to every success and mess of your life. He's just waiting for you to face Him so the two of you can face "it" together.

I noticed that David began the Scripture saying, "You have searched me, Lord, and you know me." He acknowledges that God has already searched him. However, at the end of the chapter, he says, "Search me, God, and know my heart; test me and know my anxious thoughts. See if there is an offensive way in me, and lead me in the way everlasting." *(Verses 23-24)* Although he realizes God has already searched him, now David is a willing participant in the search. He invites God to reveal to him the parts of himself that must change.

In His sovereignty, God needs neither your permission nor your help to search you. However, He still requests it. He wants you to confront your issues so you can prevent the problems from arising again. He wants you to be vulnerable, willing to lay bare on the examining table to reveal the most private parts of your soul to Him. He wants you to trust Him enough to echo David and proclaim, "Search me, God."

Introspection

I wonder if I'm living right.
It's one of my first thoughts in the morning
And one of my last at night.
Not "right" in the way that it's commonly defined
But whether I'm living the life God had in mind
Or if I'm misaligned with that for which I was designed.
I'm deathly afraid that when I make my final ascent,
I might be leaving this earth
Without ever having been present.
Because if purpose is defined as a reason for existence,
Then it's quite possible, in a sense,
Regardless the vital records in which your name was listed,
If you neglect your purpose,
Maybe you never really existed.

I wonder if you're living right,
Or instead,
Viewing things with human sight,
Questioning what God has called you to do
Because it's not that attractive to you.
But suppose
While you're sitting here trying to be sure,
God's lined up millions of people waiting on a cure
For cancer or AIDS
That's locked in the recesses of your brain.
Maybe there are some dazed and confused children
Who will remain
That way
Until you take your place before them in a classroom.
Presume there are some troubled teens and ex-cons
Who will assume
That it's impossible to turn their lives around
Because you haven't shared how you were once lost but now found.[11]

While we claim that shunning our calling is a personal decision,
Maybe God has you and another one of His children
On course for a head-on collision.
And if you've wandered off the path you're supposed to be walking,
Maybe it's not just yours
But that other person's blessing that you're blocking.

Imagine what the world would be like
Had Jesus not done that for which He was sent.
What if he did the math
And figured it wasn't a good return on his investment?
What if He decided he loved us,
But not to that extent?
What if He determined the task too inconvenient?
What if He *had* thought it robbery
To become a servant and hang from a tree?
What if He doubted His conversation with God in Gethsemane?
What if He had an extreme case of low self-esteem
And deemed Himself incapable of saving us all?
What if He was simply too afraid to answer God's call?
Now add on your other excuses
For not following your calling through,
And then ask yourself
Whether the mind of Christ actually resides in you,
Whether you truly believe in sacrifice
Or if, in theory, it just sounds nice.

I wonder if we're all living right
Or if some of us are frozen in place
Because we don't know what to do—
When there are so many ways to spend your time
While waiting for God to tell you.
Jesus was saving souls long before He hung on the cross,
Altering the lives of every person He came across.
So suppose
Each person who glimpses God through our words or deeds
Is our purpose at *that* moment
And God's way of planting seeds
For the kingdom until it breeds
A world of believers, dream conceivers,
And spiritual over-achievers.

I hope you don't feel like I'm preaching to you
Because I'm just trying to work out my own salvation—
With fear and trembling,[12]
Handing back my dying dreams to God for resuscitation.
And for those He chooses not to revive,
I'm asking Him for the strength I'll need
To perform their cremation.

I have a feeling that what you get out of this piece
Is secondary,
And the primary purpose of this poem
Is to remind me of the cross I have to carry.
Maybe God intends for this moment
To wake me from my spiritual slumber.
Because though I try to justify it,
Only He knows the number
Of hearts that would have been touched
By the things I chose not to write,
Or burdens lifted had I stepped up at an open mic.
And maybe the byproduct of this spiritual alarm clock
Is to jolt a person reading this to revolt
Against spirits of doubt, apathy, and fear,
To encourage you to persevere,
To remind you that our first calling
Is always to give God praise and glory,
To suggest that you make Him the leading man
In your life story.

Don't you wonder if you're living right?
Open your arms
And embrace the purpose God's ordained for your life
Because He stretched his arms wide for you,
Endured stripes and strife.
Know that you'll be called to give an account
When it's all said and done,
And I'd rather not have a lengthy list
Of things I had *almost* begun.
Please, keep going no matter how unlikely it seems,
Because if you chase God,
You can't help but catch your dreams.

Coming to My Senses

"Insanity: doing the same thing over and over again and expecting different results."
~ Unknown

I have always thought myself a level-headed person; however, according to the afore-mentioned informal definition of insanity, evidence suggests that I have been insane for much of my adulthood.

I came to this conclusion while digging through my old writings. I found two particularly interesting pieces, the first of which was written in 2009:

I have a love/hate relationship with my office window.

Some days, I profess my undying love for it and the light it lets into my bleak 8-hour workday. It is my connection to a world not ruled by deadlines, e-mails, and office politics. It is my meteorologist, my entertainment, and my occasional escape.

Other days, I despise the window. The sights I spy through it make me envious. I see miniature people sitting on park benches or cruising city streets in convertibles with crisp air whipping through their hair. I see trains bound for any place but here. The sights are a reminder of all that I cannot do with my weekdays, an implication that my time may never again be my own.

It is in these hate-filled moments that I curse the day the window was presented to me, a sort of peace offering to keep my groaning to a minimum. Or perhaps a bribe, given to me in exchange for the piece of my soul chained to that mahogany desk.

On such days, I wish I could press rewind on this corporate DVD—walk backward out of my office into privacy-sacrificing cubicle land, then out into the hall, down three flights of stairs, past the metal detectors, out the automatic doors, and back into a small chair with an attached desk in a classroom on the campus of Howard University, rethinking my answer to that age-old question: "What do you want to be when you grow up?"

I let the weight of that note sink in for a moment. Then I dug deeper into the box of writings and further into my past.

I discovered this, written in 2003, when I was still a new college graduate learning the ropes of a full-time career:

When I dreamed of adulthood as a child, it did not resemble this. I saw myself successful, beautiful, and happy. Whether or not I have achieved success is debatable. People say I have a good job making good money. Yet it is not as if I have an impact on the world at large. I have no passion for my work, no burning desire to rush to the office each morning.

I'm not ungrateful for what I have, but I realize it takes more than that to be happy. Therefore, I can't help wishing I could have a fresh start. I would climb back into my mother's womb and emerge with new understanding, ready to pursue all the things I now know would make my heart sing.

Two pieces—written at least five years apart and while working at two different places—saying essentially the same thing. Obviously, if I was not happy doing the work in 2003, I was not suddenly going to love it simply by changing employers a few years later. And a promotion and raise would only make it harder to walk away.

I was insane, assuming that I could somehow accept the life society said that I should have. I woke up each morning trying to squeeze my size 9 foot into a size 8 glass slipper. My career, my life, and my choices did not fit me.

But I was coming to my senses.

One New Year's Eve, the pastor preached on the subject "Doing a New You." He said we all have the power to reinvent ourselves through Jesus Christ. With the power of God working within us, we have the ability to live the life we want.

Now, when I read that first note saying I wish I could climb back into my mother's womb, I'm reminded of Nicodemus. I hear him asking Jesus: "How can a man be born when he is old? Surely he cannot enter a second time into his mother's womb to be born!" *(John 3:4, NIV)* Fortunately, that is not necessary; the Spirit can birth a new you anytime you are ready.

I am ready. It may take some time, but I am making plans to change my life so it is a better fit for who I want to be. I have come to my senses, and I don't ever intend to be the same.

Midnight

Midnight

Total eclipse.
Can't see my hand in front of my face.
A glance over my shoulder reveals
I could never find my way back.
The bleakness surrounding me
Only amplifies the darkness within.
A strange quiet
Has fallen upon the Earth,
The voices in my head
Making for horrible company.
There is an absence
Of the simple comforts
I once took for granted.
Where are You?
Have You left me
Alone in this savage world
To fend for myself?
I reach out into the abyss,
Hands groping
For pillars of hope
To steady my gait.
All I grasp
Is an epiphany:
I have never had to see You
To know that You are real.

Losing sight of myself,
I seek You with my whole heart
And find You.
You are not glowing in the darkness
As I expected.
But Your voice breaks the silence.
You whisper firmly,
Compassionately:
"Change is on the horizon."
Standing on Your promises,
I await it with bated breath.

When the Unthinkable Happens

"I just didn't think this would happen."

The gentleman who said that was speaking to a room full of people about a specific situation. However, shell-shocked by recent events in my own life, I quickly claimed his words as my own personal truth.

Some of the unexpected things were horrible situations that I never saw coming. Others were heavy moments in which the "this" I knew was possible but never believed would become real called my bluff. Either way, the circumstances were painful and difficult to comprehend. In every case, I felt blindsided by something that I just didn't think would happen.

A big part of accepting difficult life events is forgiving oneself for not anticipating them. It's easy to chide yourself for not being better prepared or for not reacting to things in a manner that hindsight now says you should have. However, denial is a stage of grief. Whether we are mourning people, places, relationships, the loss of innocence, or simply better times, grief is a part of the circle of life.

Yet even in the pain that accompanies our unthinkable moments, the words of Dr. Martin Luther King, Jr., remind us that "We must accept finite disappointment, but never lose infinite hope."

Yes, sometimes we hate the way life unfolds. We want to grab it by its collar, lay it flat on a table, smooth out its wrinkles, tuck in its sleeves, and crease it just so. At least then maybe we could try unfolding it again and see if it doesn't make something more of itself. Yet there it is, balled up into a crumpled heap on our world's floor—and we have to live with it.

When we accept finite disappointment, we recognize that our life doesn't look the way we imagined. We may not even think it remotely presentable. And we may have to wear it, as is, disheveled and homely, day in and day out. But infinite hope says that it won't always be this way. With intense scrubbing, after some time spent on the line under the scorching sun, after meeting a steaming iron, life can become presentable again. It may even wind up looking better than the first time around. Infinite hope believes in the possibilities.

When you didn't think "this" would happen and it does, keep pressing until "this" becomes "that." Until the dialogue changes from "I can't believe 'this' happened" to "I don't know how God pulled me out of 'that.'" Keep putting one foot in front of the other until you can say "I don't know how He got me from 'there' to 'here,' but I'm so much better because He did."

Keep hoping, because it has proven time and time again that it is the only cure for disappointment.

To Trayvon: An Apology

On February 26, 2012, Trayvon Martin, a 17-year-old African-American boy, was followed through his father's subdivision and confronted by a member of the Neighborhood Watch. When the situation escalated, Martin, unarmed, was shot and killed.[13] In the news reports following the incident, many argued that the fact that he was wearing a hoodie made him appear suspicious. This piece was written in 2012 following his death.

I wish I knew your name for some reason other than this. I wish it were 10 years from now and you found your way onto our television and computer screens for some great academic achievement instead, or for football dreams realized, or for some brilliant technical invention. I wish that you were not yet a household name—that you had this, your junior year, to live in the blissful obscurity that should be one's second-to-last year of high school—Friday nights with friends headed to no place in particular; Saturday mornings in front of the TV with a bowl of cereal; a spring evening with you in a tux, arm linked with a pretty girl in a dress as your mother requests just one more picture. I wish that your life had not been cut short just as it was beginning.

You crossed my mind yesterday. I was looking at the screensaver on my cell phone, smitten with the cute baby boy staring back at me. He is about your complexion, eyes bright, and cheeks chubby. In the picture, his soft brown curls are half-covered by a hoodie. He is the picture of young innocence with just a touch of cool. As I looked at him, I thought of you. I pondered the future of this black baby boy who lights up my phone and my life. I wondered what will be the "hoodie" when he reaches your age; what will be the excuse people use to justify their discomfort with his appearance.

I am currently wrapped up in the madness of March—the college basketball tournament. It is interesting that thousands of fans of all races have packed into arenas to see young men, most of them black, make magic on the hardwood. I think about what most of the black players look like off the court, how they likely appear as soon as they leave the gym following a win. How many of them wear sweatpants and... hoodies? How many of those cheering fans would sing a different tune an hour later if they saw one of those players, unrecognizable in a hoodie, walking through their gated community or some other place that they felt he did not "belong"? As happened with you, would they assume he was up to no good?

Such assumptions are the result of the quiet prejudices that most of us harbor within. Since we are well-versed in political correctness, few people would ever suspect the preconceived notions we have about persons who are different than us. Those notions may be based on previous life experiences or unwarranted stereotypes, but regardless, they cause us to size up a person before we know anything about them.

Acknowledging those biases is difficult. Most people—good people, even—cannot face that part of themselves. They think that acknowledging *any* bad part of them makes them a bad person overall. They do not realize that there is no way to chase out dark thoughts and feelings without first admitting their presence.

I am sorry for the way that some people have excused your killing. I think people's attempts to justify things are often a result of their ability to empathize with the act. It is easy for some to understand how a man could feel threatened by you for no other reason than your skin color, attire, and the fact that you were in a place he did not expect you to be—because they would have felt threatened under similar circumstances. Whether that feeling is justified does not matter. They don't want to face that part of themselves.

I'm sorry we have yet to make them face it. I'm sorry you got caught in the crossfire of a nation at war with itself. I'm sorry we have been complacent enough to believe that the election of the first black president meant you and other black men were suddenly safe, that the communities you lived in had finally welcomed you home. I'm sorry we have allowed society to make guns more tolerable in gated communities than in ghettos, or for college students to be armed instead of drug dealers. I'm sorry we still have not learned that bullets don't discriminate—people do.

I apologize to the beautiful black baby in a hoodie on my screensaver. I apologize to the talented young black man who throws on a hoodie on his way home from basketball practice. I apologize to you, shot on your way home from the store. I'm sorry that our nation keeps accepting hoodies and other excuses as justification for your deaths. I'm sorry we have not yet made it criminal to kill you.

The Saddest Eyes

(For Sybrina Fulton, the mother of Trayvon Martin)

When I look at her,
All I see are those eyes.
Hollow.
Absent anger.
No bitterness to behold.
Pain palpable.

Surely, a lifetime ago,
Those same eyes danced.
Perhaps under a starry night's sky,
With his father's arm
Draped lightly across her shoulders.
Surely they glimmered
When her child was born,
He a handful of hope
Wrapped in blue.
Surely they gleamed
At his first step,
Sparkled
At his first corny joke,
Beamed
From the stands of his first game,
Flashed
During those times in which boys will be boys.
Surely, a lifetime ago,
They were radiant,
Twinkling,
Smiling.
But the life has been drained from them,
The loss of their light
Another casualty
In this
Personal/public/national
Tragedy.
She is a woman
Who has loved and lost
As society debates
Whether her love's death
Was deserved.

Son permanently, legally
Stripped from her arms
Like generations of black women
Before her,
She stands
Tall,
Unwavering,
Courageous,
Indefatigable,
Expressionless,
Wearing,
Undeniably,
The saddest eyes.

Reconciliation
(An Open Letter to Black Men)

Brother,
If you had a dollar for each time I told you that you ain't no good,
A quarter for every criticism you withstood,
A dime for each time you were misunderstood,
Chances are,
You would be a millionaire.
I stamped you with a sign that said "buyer beware,"
Then tried to play it off like I just didn't care.
Stubbornly declared to the world
That I could do bad all by myself,
Not comprehending that our history
Can't be bound to a book on a shelf.
And while oftentimes I keep my feelings subdued,
Have you guessing
Like we're playing a round of Taboo,
I figured I would blow the whistle on these games
And make sure that you knew:
I am utterly and unapologetically enamored with you.

Because I have finally come to realize
That if I take the time to stare into your eyes,
Until I see past the disguise,
Until the many layers are peeled
And the depths of your soul are revealed,
I'd see that we're each what the other needs
In order to be healed.
I'd grasp
That every time we part, a piece of you dies,
And that I've been permanently scarred
By our hasty goodbyes.

In you,
I see my brother, cousin, father, and friend.
Because of the places we've been, you *are* my next of kin.
We were a couple
Throughout slavery, Reconstruction, and Jim Crow.
You may have to teach others your past,
But I already know.

We shared the same cramped, dirty space
On our journey across that vast ocean,
And I saw each lash of the master's whip land on you
As if it were in slow motion.
I flinched as if it had struck my own skin,
My screams resembling a screeching violin.
My arms caught you
When your broken body swooned,
Then my hands tenderly nursed your wounds
Until you were healed,
Then joined you in the cotton field.

Because you were *my* man—
When others said you were only three-fifths of a man.

We held one another up
When the blood of our sons and daughters was spilled.
When our churches and homes went up in flames,
I was the one who helped you rebuild.
I stood in your place
After they tied your neck with that noose,
Providing for our children without pity or excuse.
We linked arms to form a barricade
Against dogs and the water hose.
At Selma, you were my shield
Against the policeman's brutal blows.
At the segregated lunch counter,
Shoulder to shoulder, you and I sat.
After Vietnam,
I welcomed your warped body and mind back from combat.
I prayed for your dismal soul
When you dropped the Bible and picked up a gat.
I shouldered our family's burden
When you turned to heroin and crack.
My love was unrestricted
When you were addicted,
And even when you were wrongly
And justly
Convicted.
You closed the caskets
When our children killed one another in drive-bys.
Then, in the privacy of our home,
I wiped the tears from your eyes.

I walked through the wilderness with you
As we trekked to the Promised Land.
Every trial,
Every heartache,
We faced it hand in hand.

But this trip down memory lane
Is not to make you think you owe me anything.
I just need you to understand that what we had
Was not some simple fling.
Not even a wedding ring is symbolic enough
To represent our common struggle's worth.
So maybe we should ponder the possibility
Of our union's rebirth.

And please don't think that I'm hating on her—
For she's beautiful in her own right.
But I put in centuries of work,
And she just stepped on the scene last night.
See, I heard you when you said that I'm too hard
And just don't know how to let down my guard.
But what you seem so quick to forget
Is that you and I once faced the same threat,
That I was right beside you working up a sweat;
And that those conditions
Tend to strip away the delicate.

Now, it won't bother me terribly
If you should happen to fall in love
With someone other than me.
But my pride is crushed
When both your preference and your tendency
Is suddenly for she who is the polar opposite of me.

Brother, now that you've become every great thing
That it was said you'd never be,
Now that you're seen as more of a commodity than a liability,
Please, just don't forget about me.

The Mourning After

It is the type of horrific news that you can only process with your eyes closed. When you muster the strength to reopen them, the tears will flow.

"Self-inflicted." An ironic, unjust end for someone so caring, someone incapable of purposely inflicting pain upon anyone else.

You will brainstorm reasons, finding no justification. Yet somewhere, deep down in your soul, you will empathize. And your ability to understand something so incomprehensible will frighten you.

Your imagination will run wild, creating its own picture of the final act. The image will haunt you.

You will cry. So much so that you are sure there could not possibly be any tears left. But you are wrong. There are always more.

You will lose sleep, suddenly afraid of the dark.

You will feel an urgent need to confront issues that have been eating away at you. Freedom has never felt as crucial as in this moment.

You will engage in emotional math, counting up all the reasons he had to stay. You'll wonder in what metric system staying does not outweigh the hurt that fueled the desperation to go. You will pray that the next life will bring the peace never found in this one.

You will see him in all the old familiar places. Your eyes will squeeze shut, trying unsuccessfully to block a mental slide show whose picture repeatedly turns static well before its scripted ending.

You will consider recent smiles in contrast to the increasingly more stern disposition, eventually deciding that each face was authentic in its moment. You are all too familiar with fluctuating emotions, believing that the darkest thoughts know their place: in a quiet room when the lights go out.

The formal farewell will be overflowing with people submerged in a sea of grief. As you study the survivors, you will wonder if he knew how much he was loved. But even you realize that knowing is not synonymous with feeling.

You will consider the people in your life; could you identify others? How do you know when someone transitions from a difficult season to depression? When does it become serious? What does suicidal even look or act like? Because, apparently, you were face to face with it but didn't know.

You'll notice the long stares when people ask how you're doing. They need you to be okay. You will give the expected affirmative response, wondering if suppressing emotions to appease others is part of the problem.

You will recall an event you once attended where a man asked: "Do you know what it feels like to be hopeless?"

You will wish that hope could be bottled and sold—or better yet, distributed free of charge to the needy masses. You'll wish that peace coursed unsolicited through veins, a calm river carrying away destructive, defeatist thoughts. You'll wish that pillows were stuffed with clouds, then fluffed by the hands of God so every second of slumber was a little piece of Heaven on Earth.

You will realize that your wishes can come true, but it requires excruciating work for someone to achieve that level of liberation, and one can't get there alone.

Life will go on. Sometimes this will annoy you, but mostly, it will comfort you.

When you can put it off no longer, when the tears finally dry, you will write. The words will be slow and labored. Apropos; a long goodbye.

Finally, after this, the darkest of hours, you will pray for morning.

Don't Cry

"Don't cry for me," you would say.
If you were here today
Among these many tortured souls with emotions on display,
You would say:
"Don't cry for me."

I sit, watching the parade of broken hearts
Filing into this cold room,
Each doomed to the devastation
Of a premature and improper goodbye,
Overtaken by feelings that demand release through leaky eyes,
And I hear someone say:
"He wouldn't want us to cry."

As if tears are an enemy we must defeat,
Somehow not as natural as our heartbeat.
As if they are a dirty secret to be kept
Hidden under the cover of darkness.
As if we, made in God's likeness,
Are somehow exempt
From the same tears that Jesus wept.
As if they and all emotions must be swept
Under a carpet,
Untidy feelings serving as evidence of an unkempt mind.
So we suffer in silent sorrow,
Hiding the pain behind dry eyes,
Our buried tears now like land mines
In our hearts,
Liable to explode with just the slightest agitation,
Everyone walking gingerly through life in quiet frustration.

But why?
Hearts do not shatter quietly;
They clatter to the pit of our souls in a million clinking pieces.
Broken dreams demand to be heard,
Require mouthpieces to defend their honor and worth,
To advocate loudly and passionately for their rebirth.
And hurt feelings bear tears that must be cried—
Whether we choose to hide in private
Or in public put aside our pride,
They will not be denied.

And here I am,
Sandwiched between fellow mourners all trying not to fall apart,
My heart screaming so loudly that it shouts down my emotional levees
As if they were the walls of Jericho,
Sending a steady flow
Of tears
Gushing unconstrained.
And I feel an urge to bolt from the room,
To find some quiet, empty space to purge this pain.
But people would worry—not to mention the attention it would draw.
So as feelings gnaw at my insides,
I decide that fighting them would be my own emotional suicide.
And refusing to become an unintended casualty,
I cry myself free.

I am newly defiant.
I've tired of stifling my emotions to be compliant
With a heartless society determined to live and die
Wearing masks that grin and lie.[14]
I realize that tears are never
For the benefit of those who bear witness to their falling.
Instead, they are for the person who cries them,
Their shedding the soul's way of calling
Out to God when words cannot be found.
And I know firsthand that tears abound in limitless supply,
So I shun any notion that I save mine
For some more worthy future heartache.

For my soul's sake, I'll cry now.
I'll cry first, selfishly, for me,
Because it's what I need to be free.
And then for that crying little boy I once saw whose father
Shushed his tears with two words: "man up."
I'll cry for the years of pent-up emotions
He does not realize lie ahead.
But mostly, I'll cry for you,
All the tears that you could not shed.
I'll cry for a beautiful spirit who always put others first,
A soul immersed
In muted anguish.
I'll cry the tears I wish
You had cried for yourself.

Killing Me Softly: Keeping Quiet on Emotional Issues

"I'm not suicidal; I just don't want to be here anymore. Sometimes I feel like I'd rather not be at all."

I penned those words one emotionally grim night in 2006. I discovered them one Monday in 2012 while looking through old writings.

Reading my thoughts years later, my mind flooded with memories of what I can only describe as a difficult time. As I wrote, I was not suicidal. I gave no real thought to taking my life, but I did utter a few prayers for God to end it. And remembering in 2012 the thoughts of my 2006 self, I felt ashamed.

A couple of days after rereading that journal passage, I learned that a celebrity was dead due to an apparent suicide. I had never heard his name before, but given the way the hours unfolded between finding my old words and the reporting of his death, I was particularly saddened by the news.

In the time between these two events, within my everyday life, I listened as a woman recounted a moment when she almost took her own life, then as another described how mentally and emotionally taxing it was for her to simply get out of bed each morning, then as another confessed to being fearful that she might harm herself, and finally as yet another told me she felt she was failing at life. Four heart-wrenching stories from four different women within the course of about 36 hours.

If I dissect the last few years, I have heard similar stories from countless people I care about, but almost always after the fact. Friends have told me about times when they were seriously depressed, considering suicide, or having severe mental and emotional issues. It hurts to know that people you care about have reached rock bottom emotionally and mentally, and have gone it alone.

I am writing this piece during what has been a tumultuous season for me. Things have gone wrong in certain areas; I have failed in others. I have been hurt, I have hurt others, and so on.

Additionally, part of the reason for this season's difficulty has been my knowledge of a considerable amount of turmoil facing friends, associates, and loved ones. So as I have tried to climb out of my own emotional valleys, I have often felt guilty for even thinking about my issues when so many people's entire worlds are falling apart.

I tell you these things not for sympathy. Lord knows I was scared to even write this for fear of what people would think. However, I chose to write it anyway—for those who are wearing the same shoes as me, feeling as if they do not have a right to feel what they feel because their life is not "that bad." I write this for those who are like I was years ago—not suicidal, but no longer wanting to *be* and terribly afraid to admit it. I write this for those who have moved past that point and have quietly given serious consideration to ending life's roller coaster of pleasure and pain.

I am not sure who decided you should not talk about such things. In particular (simply because this is my reality and not because these issues don't have a broader reach), I don't know who said that if you're black or Christian or especially both that you have to suck it up and put on a happy face. Like anything swept under the rug, emotional and mental issues will eventually be found, and often when it is too late.

So many people in the world are hurting for various reasons. They carry the burden alone and it is killing them—emotionally, mentally, and sometimes physically. I can write this piece after feeling ashamed of my years-old depressed thoughts because I realize that shame is the root of the problem. There is no shame in feeling badly. There is no shame in sharing those feelings with others. There is no shame in seeking help. Only in doing so can you move from dark times to a brighter future.

I mentioned that I wrote my defeated words in 2006. It also dawns on me that less than a year after that, I was at an India.Arie concert on the night of my birthday, feeling and looking fabulous, happily singing, "I'm having a private party. Ain't nobody here but me, my angels, and my guitar, singing 'Baby, look how far we've come.'"[15]

As I sang, I remembered just how bad things had been. Realizing that the sun was so much brighter on that day because I knew what it was like to wake up to consecutive cloudy ones, I thanked God.

Don't let go when your life is overcast. I can say from experience that the sun will come out on one of your tomorrows. Please do whatever you have to do, seek whomever you need to seek, to help you not only hold on until the sunshine but to also find beauty in the rain.

Note to Self: I Think I Love You

I consider breaking up with myself every few years. Like clockwork. I regret a decision, feel guilty about something I did, dislike some aspect of my appearance, or take some failure personally—and wonder how I truly feel about Sheryl. Are we in this thing for the long-haul, or is this just an emotion-induced fling?

The answer may very well be both.

I love me. So much so that sometimes I'm a little giddy about it. Sometimes.

Yet there are other times in which the thrill is gone. And when a self-directed side eye replaces the heart-shaped pupils I spy in the mirror, I question whether I do, or ever did, love myself.

Perhaps I shouldn't. I think our culture of self-promotion would have us believe we should wake up each morning enamored with self. We perpetrate as if we should always feel like we're the best thing since sliced bread.

I respectfully disagree. Some days I get on my nerves. And in some life seasons, those days of self-annoyance accumulate into weeks. And I think that's okay.

When I consider other relationships—romantic, friendship, familial, spiritual—I realize that, as Mary J. Blige once sang, "It ain't all roses." We all know that relationships have their fair share of rough patches, so it would stand to reason that a relationship with oneself would have some volatile moments as well.

People say you have to learn to love yourself before you can love someone else. I would add that you must learn to love yourself *unconditionally* before you can love another with that same tenacity. You have to still love yourself even when you don't like you. You have to forgive yourself for your screw-ups. You have to accept you just as you are at whatever stage of life you're in. You have to keep loving you even when it's not as easy as it has been in times past.

Lorraine Hansberry's play *A Raisin in the Sun* is set in 1950s Chicago. In it, an African-American family's feud reaches epic proportions when Walter Lee, newly crowned man of the house following his father's death, makes a bad investment decision. His mistake costs the family the money they set aside to purchase a home and to fund his sister Beneatha's education. The family's hopes and aspirations, and their version of the American dream, were all wrapped up in that money. Gone.

When Beneatha turns her anger toward Walter Lee, their mother challenges Beneatha's love.

"When do you think is the time to love somebody the most?" she asks. "When they done good? … That ain't the time at all. It's when he's at his lowest…."

If we intend to love others with that resolve, we must give ourselves that same level of care. We have to dig deep, deciding to love our bowed-over selves until we can stand proud again, to love our broken selves back to wholeness, and to give tender loving care to our wounds until we are healed.

I have heard numerous church services closed with an invitation to come to Jesus. Clergy discourage waiting to "get yourself together" before accepting Christ's love because they have learned that His love is a component of self-improvement. Likewise, you can't put off loving yourself for some future time when you are "better." No, you have to embrace yourself at your worst, or in your less-than state, because that self-love is what will make you better.

Don't wait until you get a new job, lose weight, finish school, buy a house, save money, or achieve some other goal before you love yourself fully. Love yourself now—hard—even if you're down, because that is what you need. Love yourself because you will never be more worthy than you are right now.

I love myself forever and always, despite my fluctuating feelings, because I have made self-love a daily decision. I hope you will do the same.

About Face

I wanted to write fiction.
Was on a mission
To become the next Toni Morrison.
Looking to get the stories I spun
From my head into a bookstore—
But not before
Honing my craft with instruction.
Yes, I knew the odds going in:
Most grad schools had thousands of applicants
Vying for a dozen Creative Writing spots.
But I thought,
I'll just work really hard
And pray God moves these mountains for me.

So I spent weeks in preparation for the GRE.
Then recruited people to write letters of recommendation,
Which was tricky
Because I needed them to each do 10
Since that's how many schools experts said
You should try to apply.
And since each program had its own unique hoops
For you to jump through to qualify,
I didn't have the luxury
Of sending the same package to each institution.
So I wrote 10 statements of purpose
To accompany the 30 letters of recommendation,
Paid $1,200 in fees for 10 applications,
Enrolled in two different writing courses at night,
Trying to get my portfolio right.

Then I passed around drafts of my work,
Seeking other writers' advice,
Incorporating their million conflicting suggestions
With each new deadline,
Until the thoughts
Felt less and less like mine.
I'm sure I sent a different version of my 40 pages of stories
To each of the 10 schools' selection committees.

It got to the point
That the postal worker near my office knew me;
Each time I dropped off a package for another school,
She gave me an encouraging smile
Mixed with a hint of sympathy.
I guess my exhaustion was obvious.
For months, I'd been working nine hours a day
And sleeping for only three.
Each moment felt like an out-of-body experience.
I. Was. Delirious.

And after I'd given all I had within,
The replies rolled in—
A parade of no's.
Rutgers, Miami,
Hollins and Vandy—
No.
Mason and Houston,
Arizona State, Michigan—
No.
NYU and LSU—
No.

And it was a major blow
Because the only things I've ever been good at
Are writing and academics.
Bruised egos are hard enough to fix,
And Lord knows I had the names of plenty men and jobs
To throw into the mix,
But when you fail in an area
On which you've built your identity,
All you can think is:
It's me.

But as I grappled with my hurt and shrinking self-esteem,
I had to admit that God had never co-signed this dream.
Sure, I prayed for His favor to gain admittance,
But with each passing day, I began to sense
That God wanted me to make an about-turn.
But I convinced myself that each obstacle was a test or drill
To see how badly I wanted it.
In hindsight, God wanted me to discern
That I was moving contrary to His will.

He had already given me a vision
That I failed to write and make plain,
So all my efforts would be in vain
Until I completed my initial assignment.
I could lament
The death of the dream I'd carried since childhood,
Or I could embrace what He wanted me to write.
I could trust that this failure would somehow work for my good.
Novels and short stories might bear my name someday,
But for now, pursuing fiction at the expense of the truth
Is too heavy a price to pay.

I have heard that rejection
Is simply redirection—
Albeit painful, a necessary part of life.
But you can overcome it
When your identity lies in Christ.
When you accept that God knows best,
He will assure you that the story's not over yet.

Dream Chasing: Life after Death

"There should be fireworks, at least, when a dream dies." ~ Kirby Larson

I stared, unblinking, lost in those words, until my computer's screensaver eventually cued the monitor to fade to black.

There. Now it resembled the dark canyon that had swallowed my dream without fireworks or fanfare.

It's amazing how the earth continues to rotate on its axis even as your world seems to be falling apart. As devastating as my writing woes were for me, everyone and everything kept moving.

I happened upon that quote at a time when there were steady reminders of my deceased dream. Weeks before seeing it, I felt a twinge of jealousy as I came across a few writers who were like me in many ways except one: they were living a dream for which I am not destined. I also had a couple friends ask, "Hey, whatever happened with the grad school program?" I wondered how they could forget an event that was so life-changing for me. Even my doctor asked the question, following up on the reason I had given her for why I had lost so much sleep, confusing my thyroid and throwing my entire body into a tailspin as I foolishly chased a dream. I thought I made peace with myself and with God, but all these things brought back the emotions of the failure and the regret of absurd sacrifices.

However, the show goes on. And as much as we are often disturbed by this reality, we should actually take comfort in it. It means that no matter what dies—dreams, loved ones, relationships—*you* can still live. It means that the death of one thing, no matter how important, should never receive more attention than the many living, vibrant parts of you.

I now understand that there is yet another reason fireworks are inappropriate when a dream perishes. If we pulled out all the stops for a death, what, pray tell, would we do to acknowledge the resurrection?

I believe everything, through Christ, can live again. It seems we forget that. Christmas is the highlight of our year and Easter a mere afterthought. However, Christ's birth holds only a portion of the significance of His resurrection. Birth obviously represents hope, but I find it more miraculous when something dies and then lives again. Resurrection is hope on steroids, but most of us haven't even allowed it to flex its muscles.

Sadly, every dream will not live again. The key is learning the difference between *a* dream and *the* dream. I had to realize that, for me, *the* dream is writing. My dead dream is only one of several different ways I can write. It doesn't matter which of those flops — *the* dream will always live so long as I keep stringing words together into ideas.

For all of us, *the* dream is life, love, and happiness. It does not matter how many little dreams die along the way. We simply have to keep living each time that we're given the blessing of breath, and then choose to resurrect love and joy again every single day.

What things have died in your life? Mourn if you must, but be thankful that life goes on. Don't allow yourself to feel cheated that fireworks never announced that life-changing occasion. Know that a better moment, a resurrecting one, still awaits you. Save your fanfare for the finale.

The Waiting Game

I want what I want when I want it.
Call me spoiled, but you have to admit
That if your tastes and expectations are anything like mine,
You likely want Ruth's Chris value on a Mickey D's timeline.
And since I want what I want when I want it,
I recently approached God
About some things I thought He should tend to.
Because in my mind,
Some people's blessings are long overdue.

See, I know some single sisters
Who own something akin to 27 dresses;
Despite manicured hands
And professionally groomed tresses,
They are emotional messes,
Fearful that they are forever relegated to bridesmaid.
I also know some good guys who are above the games played
And opposite of the stereotypes the media has portrayed,
Yet ignored
By drama-loving women who would much rather wade
Into shark-infested waters than play it safe on the beach.
Yes, I know some folks
Whose needs are just a few steps beyond reach.
So I'm asking, when?
For the people whose bodies are racked with cancer's pain.
When for those concurrently craving
Both drug and deliverance like deserts thirst for rain?
When for the woman waiting for her husband
To finally return the love she's given?
When for the man making daily restitution to a bitter wife
For sins God's already forgiven?
When for childless middle-aged sisters
Who cry as unwed teenagers conceive?
When for saints ministering to others
What they themselves no longer believe?
When for my laid-off friends
Who now question the power of prayer?
And like those emotional messes of whom I made you aware,
I can't pretend I don't care
That my own left ring finger is still bare.

After I posed all these questions to God,
His response was not what I expected.
He told me that my attention was misdirected.
Instead of asking when a change is gonna come,
I should be focused on who He wants me to become.
I should be passing the time
With a right-now praise on my lips
For life
And the fact that my heart never skips a beat.
He said if I'm in the world rather than of the world,
If, with the Lord, one day is like a thousand years,[16]
Then I should seriously reevaluate my time down here.

God said I've been so distracted by the fact that I'm waiting,
So busy plotting, scheming, and contemplating,
That I have yet to master the lessons he wants me to learn.
When and how should be the least of my concerns.
When was the last time I gloried in tribulations?
Knowing that tribulation worketh patience,
And patience, experience; and experience, hope.[17]
God said I have to change my perspective and scope.
I need to quit pestering Him for timetables
And rest in the knowledge that He is able.
If I would seek first the Kingdom of God
And all His righteousness,
Pursue Him as passionately
As the worldly things over which I obsess,
All these things will be added unto me as well.[18]
If I'm truly a believer, I cannot continue to stress and dwell,
Or else I'm no different than the unbeliever,
Who is merely a hunter rather than a receiver.

And God said that to truly get this lesson,
I've got to look past Hollywood and beyond Capitol Hill
To find role models
Who knew what it meant to simply do His will.
Observe the lives of Joseph, Job, and Jesus
To learn the true meaning of patience and trust.
Christ longed to come down
As He endured the pain of the worst possible death.
Yet He remained on the cross,
Suffered and bled until He took His last breath.

He would not come down,
Despite the enemy's taunts and demands,
And then *waited* three more days
To rise with all power in His hands.
So now my hope is built on nothing less
Than Jesus' blood and righteousness.[19]

And Jesus is teaching me that this waiting game
Is as much about obedience as it is patience.
So I've decided to follow Him,
Despite the expense and even when it doesn't make sense.
I'll continue to jump
Regardless the number of hurdles in my path;
I'll run the marathon
Though I'd rather sprint the hundred-meter dash;
I'll dodge jabs and hooks
During round after round in the boxing ring;
I'll tee it up over and over on the golf course
'Til I perfect my swing;
I'll be the goalie on the soccer field,
Blocking each shot the devil sends my way;
I'll plow through snow-capped mountains and icy ponds
By ski, skate, or sleigh;
I'll endure the tackles on the field
And the fouls on the blacktop;
I'll dive for loose balls and swim lap after lap
Until God says stop.
I'll keep stumbling along
Regardless the balance beam's length
Because they that wait upon the Lord
Shall renew their strength.[20]

I'll wait because of countless examples
Of God's perfect timing—
Like when my car stops just seconds short of a collision,
When I'm down to my last dime
And he sends a timely provision.
I'll wait because history says He will come through.
And truthfully, I'll wait because it's the least I can do.
He waited on me through my sins and backsliding,
He waited for me to quit running and hiding.

He waited for me
To quit following every foolish impulse and whim,
He waited for me
To stop putting everything and everyone before Him.

I'm reaching down deep within
To find faith at least the size of a grain of mustard seed[21]
And enough common sense and respect
To step back and let God take the lead.
We are not called to live in distress.
Those who are truly blessed
Find peace in the fact
That we're not solely responsible for our fate,
And that all God asks in return
Is that we trust, obey, and wait.

Today I've decided
That no matter what I'm praying for or working toward,
I will wait on the Lord.

Certain Days

No one said there'd be days like this.
That amidst
The monotony of having returned to normal,
And well past the triumph of moving on,
On certain days—
The ones in which the world quakes,
Exposing a giant hole
That swallows whole
Any and every good thing—
I would type in the ten digits of your number
(From memory,
For they have long been erased from my phone).

But I do not press "call;"
Just stare at the numbers—
The sight of them,
The act of typing them,
Soothing.
As if
With each pressed digit
I left the slightest imprint on your heart,
The very act our own Morse code,
Relaying a current of thoughts and feelings
Across miles of blocked roads,
Years of bad timing,
And a chain of unfortunate events
To reach you.

In that brief moment
With your number looking back at me,
I am transported to way back then,
When we were just fools rushing in—
And suddenly,
I can breathe again.

So I inhale deeply,
Gasp enough nostalgia to last me
'Til the next time life
Brings me here.

Then I exhale
Slowly
And begin to delete the numbers
One by one,
The erasure of each digit
Bringing me back one step closer
To reality,
Until the only tangible
Connection I have to you
Is gone.

On certain days
I just need the taxing luxury
Of another goodbye.

Moment of Truth

Tell me that it isn't me,
That there is not some major flaw
Obvious to the world
Yet invisible to me.

Tell me
That it was a matter of chronology
Rather than preference;
That neither
Biology,
Psychology,
Personality,
Or physical attraction
Played a part
In your heart's
Final destination.

Tell me your decision
Was made long before we met
And I was just swept
Into the powerful current
Of your momentary doubt.
That had life played out
Differently,
You would have
Slowed long enough
For me to ride your waves with ease.

Be merciful.
Let the pieces of me
Lost in the torrent of your dark sea
Wash onto the rocky shoreline,
Gleaming in the day's sunlight
For someone else
To find.

Be gracious.
Place my world back upon its axis.
Restore my faith in gravity.
I know you have said it before,
But recurring themes make me wonder.

Please convince the pesky, insecure
Part of me
That's no longer sure.
I suspect
But have no real proof.
In this moment of truth,
Tell me
That it's not me.

Mute

Words are complex lovers.
Seductive, exhilarating,
Eloquent, expressive,
Wildly freeing
When you give voice to them.
But sometimes,
After you've left the warmth of their embrace,
They can unknowingly betray you.
Despite the best intentions,
Their mere utterance
Makes your heart a social experiment,
Your emotions fodder for curious conversation,
And your thoughts
The very rocks the crowd will later use to stone you.

In the interest of self-preservation,
I take unspoken words that have swelled
Into a massive tumor on my tongue
And shove them back down my throat,
An attempt to choke the feeling out of them.
Rather than call it what it is,
Determined to starve the subject
Until the point is moot,
I press mute.

Many unexpressed words, lacking purpose,
Are destined to perish.
For some,
A Higher Voice will verbalize their truth.
Yet other muted words experience neither.
Those tormented, silenced remarks
Prick your insides mercilessly,
Begging release.
And by His grace,
If they bear any healing or redemptive power,
Eventually,
Those words will stubbornly break free.
He will give them a platform to breathe.
And your muted, sufferable soul
Will finally be at liberty
To speak.

Restless Nights

When the day's curtain closes
And my mask is removed,
When the lights shut off
And all the world sits still,
I lie down in the pit of feelings
That this empty bed has become.
Arms wrapped tightly around my pillow,
Mind cuddling thoughts of you.
Limbs entwined with sheets,
Emotions entangled with you.
I have yet to test its hypothesis,
But my heart insists
That the best sleep
Is lying next to you.

Finally
Surrendering to slumber,
I dare to dream
That maybe,
Just maybe,
You're thinking of me, too.

When Dreams Collide

Each dream means the world to me. Yet sometimes I wonder if they are speeding toward one another like two freight trains destined to collide. Aboard one: a handsome, loving man and 2.5 children. The other is occupied by words; lots of them, bouncing wildly from wall to wall and finally piling up on a stage in the center of the car.

Neither exists yet; both still visions forming in my mind. However, even in their infancy, they appear in competition with one another. As I try to sort it out, each is gaining steam, tooting its horn, preparing to outrun the other.

They say you can have it all, just not all at once. Given my age and the fact that both are lagging, I wonder what would happen if these two dreams ran neck and neck for a while but then ultimately forced me to pump the brakes on one of them? Could this fear of eventually having to choose be the very reason I have not given my all in pursuit of either dream?

As a chronic overachiever, I have been known to sacrifice a lot—too much—trying to be great. It has become more of an issue now that I realize my career lacks fulfillment. My free time is dedicated to writing and church and social activities. This results in less mixing and mingling. But how likely am I to meet the man of my dreams if I'm busy chasing other dreams?

Additionally, once love arrives, I want to give it my best. What will my best look like in a relationship? Will I write when I should cuddle, or turn down quiet time with my significant other in order to attend a poetry event? I wonder if I will approach important conversations just as Darius Lovehall did in *Love Jones*, with one curt phrase: "You're wrecking my flow."

I'm reminded of a scene in another African-American classic, *Love and Basketball*. Sweethearts Quincy and Monica are each on their college basketball teams. One night, Monica, on the verge of her big break, has to decide whether to return to her dorm in time for curfew or stay out with Q to discuss his family problems. Forced to choose between her two loves, Monica opts to chase her lifelong basketball dream. Her decision leads to a break-up. I have to wonder how many times I would fail such a test.

I am also curious whether men only like ambitious women to a point. Is a lady's hustle more attractive when it doesn't interfere with a man's view of the ideal relationship? Are Jay-Z and Beyoncé seemingly happy because they are *both* entertainment moguls? How important was it that they each achieved solo success before the relationship? If they were both broke and struggling to pursue their dreams, would her ambition have been a problem, particularly when they decided to have a child?

I was brunching with lady friends once and shared that I worry how love will fit into my life plan. Mind you, I don't *have* a plan, but I suspect it may unfold in a nontraditional way. I wonder how many men will be open to that. The girls assured me that there are men who will be accepting. Yet a while later, one of those friends discussed the matter with her boo and he confirmed that it would take a different type of man to wife me. And those words sounded eerily similar to some I once heard from a man I was seeing.

I'm no Bey, but I know that my dreams don't fit into normal business hours. That, along with the hectic schedule I keep, makes the precious babies that melt my heart seem unattainable. If I have trouble maneuvering my life solo, how will I manage a party of two or more?

Yet that's only one side of my fear. The other is that the complete opposite will occur. What if I fall head over heels as I've done before and lose myself? Will I sacrifice my writing in the name of love? And is the probability of that the very reason God has not yet sent "him"?

Or maybe I've grown since I loved last. Perhaps it won't be all consuming; instead, it will leave space for me to breathe, write, recite, and still exist as "me" apart from the "we." Maybe God, in His infinite wisdom, designed things so that my two dreams will merge rather than collide—husband and writing possibilities both appearing on the scene at a time in which all my previous experience and desire for both will ensure I value each enough to give them both what they need. Hopefully He'll send a husband who manages to strike a balance between pushing me to greatness and pulling me back when ambition threatens to take too much from me and our family. Maybe we'll make beautiful brown babies together and craft a lifestyle that works for us.

Or maybe it will be more difficult than that. Perhaps both dreams can coexist, but I'll be forced to make choices day after day, year after year throughout my life. I don't know. What I *do* know is that I can write, and well. But do I know how to be with a man? Sometimes I think yes, but my track record is questionable. And will the right man ever appear? The jury's still out on that as well.

So no matter how loudly my heart screams for love, I can't help but follow the whisper of a prudent mind telling me to write. However, if I can't quiet that other internal organ—the shrieking, persistent one—is it even worth it?

Looking for Love

Where is he?
Needle in a haystack.
Like looking for a contact lens in the pitch black of night,
Straining through impaired sight
In search of a million-dollar check in a landfill of bills.
I feel
Like a Forty-Niner chasing gold,
But at least then I'd know how to narrow my search.
Instead, I'm perched
Atop a crumbling foundation of faith,
Hoping my proximity to God will make
His omnipresence and omniscience rub off on me,
So I'll be exactly where I need to be
With the presence of mind to discern what I see.

And all the while,
The world's steady cracking jokes
And offering clichés
About better days,
Like this is as simple as *Where's Waldo*.
But they don't know my struggle.
Because until you've smuggled hope like dope
Past skeptical security on each leg of your life journey,
Each time lugging more baggage
And paying an increased boarding fee,
You can't appreciate
That sometimes,
It feels like the hunt for Osama bin Laden.
So maybe I should call in the Navy Seals
Or put out an All-Points Bulletin—
Except not only can I not tell them where he's going,
I don't even know where he's been.
I can offer no physical description.
No personality traits, no birth date.
Neither government nor nickname.

No idea of the people from whence he came.
No clue of his past deeds,
No hint of his wants or needs.
Absolutely no leads.
Because I'm searching for someone I haven't met yet.
The odds are so low no sane person would make this bet.
Forget one in a million; the census says it's one in 7 billion.
People tell me, "You don't need a man,"
But what they don't understand
Is I'm looking for a who as a means to the what.
Yes, I've wished for a special someone,
But
I really just want what my heart's been dreaming of.
Quite simply, I'm looking for love.

Now, there were times in my past
When I thought, at last,
I'd found love.
But my mind is taunted by flashbacks
Of fish caught and thrown back.
Counterfeits and misfits.
Mirages in the midst
Of my emotional desert.
Men putting up barrages
Against potential hurt,
Which, ironically, caused *me* harm.
False alarms.
Watered-down love,
Deprived of
All nutrients and flavor.
Love devoured when it should have been savored.
Love built on so many lies it couldn't be saved by the truth.
Love birthed in the innocence of youth,
Too naïve and fragile to withstand the test of time.
Love shared, though I've demanded everything else in life be all mine.
God's sacred Love,
Desecrated for our own selfish designs.

I'm looking for love
But I'm convinced it's not looking for me.
The chase has left me short of breath,
Hope on empty.
Maybe
It's time to call it quits.
I'm given to spiritual fits,
Regularly telling God,
"I give up, I give in;"
No longer sure what I believe in.
I fall to my knees
Pleading with the man above.
Lord, help!
I'm tired of looking for love.

Revelation

I had laid my heart bare,
Begged God in prayer
For the who I sought as a means to the what.
But He always seems to rebut.
He said I'd been looking for love
In all the wrong places,
In unstable arms and unfamiliar faces,
In cold spaces with no traces of love.

Some people spend their whole lives
Looking for what's right in front of them.
In my hunt for this mythical man I could only name as "him,"
I spent mine
Seeking that which was already *inside* of me.
Because I'd been led to believe
That you can't feel what you can't see.

But in a brief moment of clarity,
I realized
I could search from sea to shining sea,
Skip across the pond,
Then land on the sands
Of the Mother Land,
But if it was love I was chasing,
I'd have to spend more time embracing
The girl facing me in the mirror.
And to see her clearer,
I had to draw nearer
To the One who loved me first,
Who claimed me at my best and my worst.
Become immersed
In the greatest love story ever written,
Learn of one so smitten
That He could actually claim love *before* first sight,
Since He molded each part of me by hand until I was just right.

Read about the kiss of life with which I was conceived,
Hear the sweet nothings whispered
When He promised never to leave,
Discover His unselfish choice to give
His own life that I might live.

And as I stand in complete awe of His perfection,
I can't help but regard the object of His affection.
I'm impressed by a mind that studies to both understand and impart,
A heart that aches and rejoices for its neighbors,
A spirit that labors to follow its Father's direction,
A chocolate-dipped complexion,
Hips that tantalize,
Twinkling eyes,
And a smile that is syrupy sweet.
Why worry when I'll meet my dream man
When no one can love me more than God can?
Another love will come when it best fits into His plan.
Besides, I'll never truly believe
That anyone else can love me
If I haven't first conceived it for myself.
I'm too precious to share,
Require the utmost care,
Deserve for a man to give me his absolute best.
If I want to be respected and spoiled like a princess,
Then I can't treat myself as anything less.
So I'll practice what I preach
Each day, as I heap
Affection upon the lady who's walked with me day in and day out,
Until I teach myself what love's all about.

I was looking for a who as a means to the what,
But—God is love.
With Him, it's not a question of either/or;
Not a matter of which comes after or before;
I have both the who and the what,
And that's more than enough.

In the Middle of It

Current location: the middle of it.

"It" is, well, everything. Life, career, faith, hope, love—I'm smack dab in the middle of it all. I have accomplished some short-term goals and made significant progress in certain areas of life. However, when it comes to a final destination, I'm clueless. So right here in the middle of it, far from where I began but God knows how far from where I'm going, I find myself unraveling.

While freaking out, I happened upon a familiar story in the Bible *(Exodus 14, NIV)* about a group that found itself in the middle of an "it" of its own. The children of Israel fled from Pharaoh's oppressive reign, following the direction of God as given to Moses, on their way to a land overflowing with milk and honey. In the middle of their journey—beyond their place of bondage but not yet in the Promised Land—they were camped out near the sea. With their former oppressors pursuing them, the Israelites were sandwiched between water and a hostile enemy. Trapped and certain they would die, they freaked out. Surely God had not brought them all that way only to die?

During their breakdown, God said to Moses, "Why are you crying out to me? Tell the Israelites to move on. Raise your staff and stretch out your hand over the sea to divide the water so that the Israelites can go through the sea on dry ground." *(Verses 15-16)*

Moses complied and God "drove the sea back with a strong east wind and turned it into dry land. The waters were divided, and the Israelites went through the sea on dry ground with a wall of water on their right and on their left." *(Verses 21-22)*

I've read that story several times but gave little thought to what it might be like to walk with a wall of water to your right and another on your left. I always assumed I would just walk across like everyone else. But my history says otherwise. If I approached that sea as I have my writing and life in general, I would probably start across it very slowly, then get to the middle of the dry land that God paved in the center of a sea, finally *grasp* that I was standing in the middle of a sea, and flip out.

Foolish, right? A better person would reason that since God was both powerful and caring enough to part the seas in the first place, He would make sure to hold the waters back until that person made it safely to the other side. It would not matter that they could see, hear, and feel the spray of the water on either side of them; they would just marvel at God's omnipotence, trust His plan, and keep it moving.

Some of us are in the middle of some monumental "its." We have made progress in jobs, relationships, and dreams only to get to the middle of it, realize just how fragile the situation is, notice our former oppressors of insecurity and doubt hot on our trail, and flip out. But it makes no sense to walk halfway down a path that God miraculously paved specifically for you, then lie down and throw a tantrum.

You may not know exactly where you're going. You may be frightened by the sights and sounds surrounding you. But keep walking. The fact that God set you free and brought you this far, that He's *visibly* moving obstacles out of your way at present, is reason enough to trust Him.

What are you in the middle of? Have you stopped to freak out or breakdown? Stop crying, keep moving. You may not be able to clearly see your Promised Land, but trust that the way has been made clear.

Trust Issues

You don't realize the depth of your trust issues until you are in a relationship.

In your single state, you float through life leisurely, downplaying your tendency to flinch at the hint of an unexpected current or to bolt upright at the slightest sound.

A relationship takes you below the surface. Your complete reliance on another being, for anything at all, submerges you. The determinant for how that immersion causes you to feel—helpless or carefree—is your level of trust.

Our trust issues do not just drop out of the clear blue sky. They have origins: someplace, someone, somehow, sometime, long ago. Broken promises, buried truths, bold-faced lies, betrayed confidences, belated appearances, brief lapses in judgment, burdened hearts, the best intentions curtailed by human limitations. They all contribute to our inability to trust. And sometimes, the disappointments heaped upon us by other people are only part of the story. The prologue is our own personality, a need to control and do everything for ourselves. When we are no longer a solo project, when we invite someone to walk this life journey with us, those trust issues materialize as we struggle to release the hurts of the past and to relinquish total control in the present.

I did not realize the depth of my trust issues until I began to grow in my relationship with God. I like to think that I am easygoing; controlling is not a word that I would typically use to describe me. However, if I am honest, my ability to go with the flow is often relegated to situations in which the stakes are not high. Yet when it comes to those aspects of life that matter most and can cause ripple effects into other areas, I have a firm opinion on the right way, time, and place to do it.

Interestingly enough, when it comes to dating, I have always said I don't like punks. I am completely uninterested in pushovers. I suppose I have always known that I have a strong will and do not want a man who will let me walk all over him.

Though this is a pre-requisite for my future love, most of the complications to my relationship with God are due to the fact that, um, He ain't no punk! I cannot push Him around, cannot force Him to concede to my every demand, cannot put Him on my deadlines, and cannot convince Him to go against His will. While He is giving and compassionate and sacrificial, the closer we become, the more He expects me to just trust Him.

It really should not be hard. God has declared on several occasions that He would never leave nor forsake me (*Hebrews 13:5*), that He is not a man that He should lie (*Numbers 23:19*), and that He has plans to prosper me (*Jeremiah 29:11*). And He doesn't just talk a good game; He has proven Himself trustworthy. I know what He has done for others, and His track record in my life is the very reason I am with Him in the first place. I have every reason to trust Him, but after a history of putting my hope in the wrong things (sometimes my own power being one of them), I occasionally struggle to keep the faith.

As I type this, Etta James has coincidentally made an appearance on my playlist. She is passionately asking her love to trust her:

"Trust in me in all you do. Have the faith I have in you…. Why don't you trust in me? Why don't you come to me when things go wrong? Cling to me, and I'll be strong."[22]

The song is an earnest plea, a prayer. It reminds me how much it frustrates and hurts the person who loves us when we are unable or unwilling to offer them our trust. They may understand when they have done something to break it in the past, but oftentimes, perfectly innocent people and untainted relationships bear the brunt of our trust issues. We not only force them to pay for others' wrongs but also to submit to our dictatorial reign. Neither is fair.

Deal with your trust issues. Don't allow them to fester, for they will only seep into the most beautiful relationships in your life, leaving a stain that is nearly impossible to remove.

No Looking Back

It is one of my biggest regrets. Standing at a fork in my relationship road, looking back and forth between the past and a possible future, weighing the odds of each, I snubbed the future and embraced the past. Never mind that the past had failed before and was destined to fail again. Forget that the future was what I said I wanted. Maybe I chose the familiar, recurring pain of the past rather than subject myself to potentially worse pain in the future. And after the past had broken my heart in the present as well, I turned to that potential future, and it was no longer a possibility.

When I was younger, I was troubled by the fate of Lot's wife during the destruction of Sodom and Gomorrah in the Bible. When Lot, his wife, and his two daughters were spared, the instructions given to them were "Flee for your lives! Don't look back and don't stop anywhere in the plain!" As they traveled, "Lot's wife looked back, and she became a pillar of salt." *(Genesis 19:1-29, NIV)*

That seemed so cruel to my young mind. A pillar of salt for glancing over your shoulder? I wondered if I were in her shoes, would I have also looked back and become a pillar of salt? I'm not sure why she looked back. It could have been curiosity, or longing for the life she was leaving behind, or fear of the unknown lying ahead. Regardless the reason, she looked back.

The regretful fork in my relationship road taught me many things, particularly that when we look back to negative situations from which we have been delivered, we are turning ourselves into a pillar of salt. An obsession with the past, either dwelling on the wrong done to you or longing for something you left, will not let you enjoy your present or walk into your future.

There are a few reasons why:

One look is never enough. Whatever Lot's wife saw when she looked back would have only teased her curiosity or desire. She would have needed more, and she would have looked back again and again. As she kept looking over her shoulder with every few steps, her family would have realized that…

Looking back slows you down. Have you ever watched a horror flick with someone who likes to yell at the TV? What do they say to the chick running in high heels through the empty parking lot? "Don't look back, girl! Run!" You might be able to trot slowly while stealing backward glances, but that trot will never evolve into a brisk walk or sprint as long as you keep trying to see what is behind you. Thus,

You can't look back and move forward at the same time. You need to be able to see where you're headed. You can't do that if you're looking back. You'll find yourself either colliding with something, heading in the wrong direction, or stagnant like someone running on a treadmill.

The fate of Lot's wife was not cruel. God knew what we often refuse to accept. A fixation on the past can paralyze you. And by the time you finally decide to let go, there is no telling how many opportunities you may have missed in the present and how many you're on the verge of ruining for the future.

Here's to moving forward!

Hellos and Goodbyes

When my grandmother bid this world goodbye, I was fortunate in that I knew it was coming. As I awaited the official word, my sister and I shared a long telephone conversation. We discussed our grandmother's inevitable passing and other family news; a little random this, a lot of random that.

At some point, our conversation shifted to my sister's baby boy.

"Come tell Auntie hi," she said to him.

I expected some cooing and babbling, but certainly nothing resembling the actual word "hi." It had been at least a month since I had last seen him, and I foolishly assumed he temporarily paused development during our time apart.

But there it came, a little voice booming a simple-yet-lovely phrase through the phone: "Hi." I smiled and cheered, my spirits momentarily lifted.

I would later learn that my grandmother was gone and would piece together that she likely passed minutes before this surprise greeting from my nephew. Her closing remark was followed by his salutation. As she bid us farewell, he, a new generation, said hello. The end of her story was also the beginning of a new family chapter.

Whether expected or completely out of the blue, goodbyes are a necessary part of life. In some instances, like in the case of my grandmother, the departing party is in need of some long-awaited rest. Other times, relationships and people have run their course and there must be a parting of ways. Occasionally, departures are abrupt and illogical, troubling the minds and shattering the hearts of those left behind.

Sometimes goodbyes are final, and we must make our peace with the end. Still other times, farewells are temporary and would be more appropriately phrased "until we meet again." Regardless, they are disappointing and painful as we can't help but mourn what once was.

My nephew's sweet voice reminded me that even in the midst of our goodbyes, there will always be hellos.

As long as we're still here and breathing, we have to believe in both the inevitability and the power of hello. It heals what has been broken, breathes life into that which is lackluster, and strengthens our faltering faith.

It's okay to mourn when you say goodbye. Take as much time as you need. But remember that there is a circle of life. In the midst of hurtful farewells, cling to the promise of an upcoming hello.

Daybreak

Daybreak

In the distance,
A ray of light peeks out of the clouds.
The darkest hour now behind me,
Your light beckons me
Forward,
Promising
The latter will be greater than the former,[23]
That my best days have yet to come.
Eyes focused on You,
Mind blocking out any lingering darkness,
I step forth
With slow confidence.
Change is on the horizon,
I await You with bated breath.

Re-Routing: Divine Detours

I have newfound respect for Google Maps.

One day, I plugged in a friend's address, scanned the instructions, and then muted the verbal play-by-play. I knew how to get to the city she lived in, so I figured I would head that way and consult the directions again when I was closer.

As I took the ramp for the Beltway (D.C.'s expressway), I realized I was headed south when the GPS wanted me to go north. "That's odd," I thought. "I always go south."

Since the Beltway is one big circle, I was not concerned. I figured my destination was halfway around the circle, so I could hit it from either direction. Maybe the GPS route was a couple minutes shorter, but it wouldn't make a big difference. The system would just re-route in my chosen direction.

Wrong. The GPS re-routed alright. It wanted me to get off at the next exit and make a U-turn. Already late, I disregarded it.

I passed a couple of exits, still ignoring it. It kept re-routing, still trying to get me to turn around.

"Geez," I thought. "You *really* want me to go that way." I was curious but refused to follow its instruction. "Ain't nobody got time for that."

Eventually, the system accepted that I was not going to turn around and it gave me a new route that allowed me to stay the course I had already begun. However, it wanted me to get off the expressway halfway through my trip, take a few local roads for a couple miles, and then get back on the expressway headed in the same direction. What?

When I found myself facing a sea of brake lights, I understood. There was an accident ahead. From the very beginning, Google Maps had tried to save me from the inconvenience by suggesting the less-obvious route. When I was too hard-headed to listen, it worked with my chosen direction but still offered an alternate route around the back-up.

Finally convinced of its reasoning, I followed the system as it led me around the accident. When I made it back onto the expressway, all was clear.

Sometimes we're so confident that we know how to get someplace that we ignore alternate routes from navigation systems that have more current information than we do. I'm known to consult a GPS when I'm already stuck in traffic because I want it to guide me around it. Yet it never occurred to me that the GPS was proactively trying to avoid the congestion altogether.

Life can sometimes resemble my trip around the Beltway. We think we know the way to our desired destination so we take off. We're technically going the right way, but we don't realize that we're not taking the fastest route. God nudges us quietly, suggesting that we turn around. We disregard Him because we're comfortable with the way that we already know. We're wearing our knowledge and previous experiences like blinders, blocking out His wisdom. Other times we ignore Him because we don't want to lose time by turning around.

Thankfully, whether we are ignorant or stubborn (or both), God is like Google Maps. At first, He asks us to make a U-turn. The further we advance, the more He re-routes. When we reach the point that we can no longer turn around, He gets creative and offers an alternate route. Even when we have come to a complete standstill, He still points out a detour that we had not considered. It is a lifeline, leading us around the obstruction we were so determined to meet head-on.

I'm thankful that God is able to get us to our destiny at any cost. We may arrive later than planned, but if we will listen to His voice and heed His instruction, we will still arrive sooner than if we had been left to our own devices. And when we do, we will have a newfound faith in Him and His plan for our lives.

Almost Doesn't Count

One night as I was driving home, I had to thank God that "almost" doesn't count.

I was sitting at a four-way stop, awaiting my turn. My side of the stop sign had two lanes. I was headed straight while the van beside me was turning right. We had both arrived at the stop sign at the same time, so as the van made its turn, I pulled out into the intersection.

I was looking to my left to make sure nothing was coming from that direction. As my head turned to the right, I saw bright headlights. An SUV, which apparently had not been able to see me due to the van turning in its direction, was coming straight for me.

I screamed. I laid on the horn. Then I pressed the brakes.

It was the wrong thing to do. I instantly knew that I should have gunned it instead. The SUV came to a screeching halt at the same moment I did. Our vehicles were inches from one another, each of us staring in dumb disbelief at the person with whom we had almost collided.

Finally regaining my composure and a modicum of sense, I placed my foot on the gas and cautiously drove the final feet to my home.

After I parked, I got out of the car and walked around to the passenger side. I half expected to see a dent. I placed my hand against the spot of the almost-collision, double-checking for scratches. Of course there were none. My car was clean as a whistle. It's just that I had come *so close*. So close that I could not believe I had escaped the incident unscathed.

As I considered how dangerously near disaster I was on the road, I realized how perilously close we can come to catastrophe in other life situations. Our jobs, our relationships, our finances, our physical health, our mental stability, and our emotional well-being are sometimes within an inch of misfortune.

How often have we almost collided with things and people who had the power to completely undo our entire worlds? How many times have we done the wrong thing or responded in the wrong way, putting ourselves even more in harm's way? But how many of us know that as close as we have come to wrecking our lives, we somehow escaped tragedy by a thumbnail? How many of us understand what it is like to stand back and wonder how we made it through such a potentially damaging situation with absolutely no scratches or scars? No one else knows how close we came to forfeiting everything. The only evidence of our foolishness exists in our memories.

We almost lost it all. We almost broke down. We almost went crazy. We almost threw in the towel. Our worlds almost exploded. Our faith almost ran out. Our hope almost disintegrated.

But it didn't. We didn't. God didn't allow it.

For those moments, when grace and mercy are the only explanation for how you made it safe and sound, neither battered nor bruised, but tougher and wiser, with yet another opportunity to try again, we all should thank God that "almost" doesn't count.

Gratitude

Dear Lord,
It's been brought to my attention
That I mostly make prayers of petition
Rather than of thanksgiving and submission.
Every time we speak,
I have a list of protests and requests
And usually,
I'm not asking for peace or patience to withstand tests.
I'm ashamed to admit
That my words of thanks are many times
Few and far between.
And they often come as if on cue,
So you might wonder if they're words I really mean.
Sometimes I say "thank you" with no deliberation,
Possibly without any true appreciation.
And when I became aware of my lackadaisical attitude,
I had to take a few minutes to express my gratitude,
Just in case my future moments should ultimately cease to be.

So thank you
For the time and care you spent crafting and fashioning me.
I'm thankful that you looked down on me
And saw that it was good.
Thank you that you love me
Way more than anyone could,
More than anyone in their right mind would,
So much more
Than even you know you should.
More than a fat kid loves cake,[24]
Lord, you love just for love's sake—
A love that man can emulate
But not duplicate.
More than the love described
In the wedding vows we make:
In sickness and in health,
In poverty and in wealth,
Truly for better or for worse,
Beyond the funeral and hearse,
Because not even in my death
Will we part.

In Heaven, we'll enhance what on earth we did start—
Continuous praise and worship
When we meet face to face.
Thank you
For that promise
To those who run this Christian race.

Lord, thank you for the fact
That you continue to cut your children some slack.
You enable our one step forward,
Then pardon our two steps back.
Thank you for forgiving my distant and recent past,
The 33 years' worth of sins I've amassed
And those committed in the 24 hours that just passed.
All while knowing *that* sin would surely not be the last.

I thank you for life lessons
That taught me your healing power
And showed me that even when tears fall,
Every hour on the hour,
Your gentle hand can wipe them away.
And your Son can cast His rays
On even the gloomiest days.
Thank you that spring and summer
Always follow winter's harsh cold,
That through emotional earthquakes,
Your touch has steadied my soul.
Thank you that when people walked out
And things fell apart,
You were the source of the joy in my heart.

If I had ten thousand tongues,
I couldn't thank you enough.
But really, I need ten thousand minds—
Or just one with enough
Wisdom to know to thank you
Even when the going gets tough,
And to thank you just as much for the things you've taken
As for the things you give,
And insight to thank you because if justice was done,
I'd be deemed unfit to live.

And I need ten thousand hearts—
Or one clean one
To value people and blessings more than stuff,
To smooth out the many pieces of me
That this cruel world has made rough,
And to reciprocate even a percentage
Of the love
You've shown us.

Thank you, Lord,
And thank you again.
Thank you for all you are and have been.
Thank you for now and thank you for before.
Thank you, thank you, and then thank you once more.
I'll take a trip around the world
And say thank you in any language
That you're in the mood to hear:
Gracias, merci, mahalo, dankeschoen.
I just want to make a sweet sound in your ear.

Lord, I think you probably get the picture
That "thank you" should be a permanent fixture
In my mind, in my heart, and on my tongue—
The staple of every prayer prayed and song sung.
But my humanity and selfishness limit me.
There will be countless times that I forget to thank thee.
But please, consider this
Thank you
To the infinite degree.

I Want It All Back

My baby nephew has learned a new word. I made the discovery one day as I watched him at play with his older cousin. I sensed my nephew's frustration as he watched another child becoming quite comfortable with his toys. Then, shortly after taking a stroll about the room in his father's shoes, he looked on longingly as his cousin slipped them on his own feet. And finally, when my nephew grabbed a broom and his cousin attempted to pull it away from him, it happened. Face tense, cheeks flushed, and fists clenched around the broom handle, he screamed: "Mine!"

There was nothing more to be said. The adults present saw no need to give my nephew a lesson on sharing. He had been sharing quietly, but at some point, he realized that he was repeatedly getting the short end of the stick. And he'd had enough.

We can reach a point in life in which it would behoove us to stop allowing people and situations to push us around. We can come through some difficult seasons and heartbreaks in which we're stripped of important things that we typically take for granted: happiness, peace, hope, love, and gratitude. We can wake up one morning and find that, after enduring life's rough patches, we are only a shell of the vibrant person we once knew and loved. But will we have the courage to demand it all back?

Things happen. Life does not go as planned. We suffer hurt and disappointment. It is perfectly acceptable to deal with those issues, to process that which has happened, and to feel the associated emotions. However, after a while, we should tire of being controlled by circumstances and people. We may not be able to regain material possessions, or to reincarnate lost loved ones, or to resurrect dead relationships; but we can always reclaim our joy, peace, and hope. We can make the decision to let go of the hurts of our pasts and to move forward believing that the future will bring better days.

Life may have dealt you some difficult moments, but what have you done now that those times have passed? Are you still sulking, or have you brushed it off? Have you resigned to live in quiet suffering, or are you ready to stand up for yourself? When will you get angry enough to scream "Mine!"? When will you declare that you want it all back?

How I Knew Writing Was "The One"

Lauryn Hill said, "Hip hop started out in the heart." My writing had its origins there as well.

At any given moment, my feelings decide to pitter patter across my heart—baby emotions trying to find their place inside of a complex woman. Preoccupied, I let them play unattended.

Some of those feelings, either fickle or attention-starved, fizzle and eventually die. Others, the clingy type, hang on for dear life. They mature and take the road less traveled, journeying to my head. There, they conspire with the running narrative that is my thought life. And as my feelings turn themselves over and over in my mind, the quarters become cramped and noisy.

Quiet and freedom comes in writing. The act of choosing words and formulating sentences sets my caged thoughts and emotions free. And that's what love does, right? It liberates us, saves us from ourselves, adds the pretty to our good, bad, and ugly until they all combine to make us beautiful.

A fellow blogger once requested a topic straight out of the *Brown Sugar* screenplay. In the movie, Sidney is a hip hop head and journalist who always begins her artist interviews with the same request: "Tell me when you fell in love with hip hop." Similarly, my blogger friend asked me to share when I fell in love with writing.

It seems simple enough. The implication: if you're not some new kid on the block chasing a fad, you'll know when you fell. Well, my name's not Donnie Wahlberg, but I honestly can't remember a specific time, place, or event. I've always written; I've had a relationship with words since I started reading. Just as little girls put on make-up and heels to imitate their mothers' outer beauty, I put pencil to paper trying to mimic the writers who penned words that touched my insides. It's been a challenging relationship full of starts and stops, quickened pulses and lackluster performances, swelling hearts and hurt feelings, but if I ever walk away, when the thoughts and feelings become too much, it calls for me. Surprisingly, back under its spell, slave to its demands, somehow, I am free again.

And that's what God does, right? He liberates us, serves as our gateway to our true selves, multiplies our goodness, converts our flaws, extracts beauty from our pain.

So I suppose my attraction to writing is only natural, as I'm drawn to it for the same reasons I cling to Him. Maybe I find God at that place where Bic glides across white paper, at that moment when letters appear on a blank screen.

Writing is my way of accepting that overthinking and over-feeling have always been the essence of who I am. And every time I write, I realize the craft is actually God's gift to me—our secret meeting place, my way of signing my own freedom papers again and again, His way of making me beautiful.

I guess I fell in love with writing the moment I gave myself permission to love me.

Terrifyingly Beautiful

Blank page.
I am staring at a breathtaking clean slate,
Intimidated by its empty expanse.
Creative thoughts swimming through my head
Crash into ever-looming self-doubt.
Mind is unleashed but fingertips frozen.
The invisible struggle
Of excitement staring down apprehension.
The tug of war between creation and critique,
The irony of a reserved person
Finding healing through revealing.
Beauty versus terror, engaged in a shouting match.
I listen quietly, an unqualified adjudicator
With bias toward each side.
Finally,
Unable to tolerate their raucous voices vying for my attention
And fearful that the fight will turn bloody,
I give confidence the floor,
Allow her the space and time to silence the skeptic.
She is soft-spoken, calm, assured.
Deep breaths precede key strokes.
My heart on a page,
For your reading pleasure.

Hot mic.
As I peer out at the crowd,
I am floating on adrenaline and wading in dread.
I find freedom in the words tumbling from my lips,
But vulnerability bears a ball and chain all its own.
I have never been more sure of my ability,
Yet keenly aware of my deficiencies.
This, the perfect platform to purge,
Can be as intimidating as a judge's chambers.
For there are eyes, dozens of pairs,
Some expectant and curious,
Others bored and challenging,
All staring at me.
I am both motivated and intimidated
By this audience that hangs on my every word
And detects my every stumble.

The mic was love at first rhyme,
But each time
We join together,
I'm reminded that it has the power
To break my heart.
So I love it
And hate the power I've surrendered to it.
I spit with authority,
But it's an act of submission to the One who called me.
So I tap into Him,
Ask that His strength be made perfect in my weakness.
Prayer precedes recitation.
Heart on a stage,
For your listening pleasure.

Each time I write or step up to a mic,
I try to gingerly untie the bow wrapped around this gift
Like someone trying not to detonate a bomb,
Because I know the explosive powers within.
I am stunned and flattered to have been chosen,
Yet overwhelmed by the responsibility.
I am uncomfortable with my imperfection,
And simultaneously petrified by the best of me.
How terrifyingly beautiful.

I Give Myself Away

I am not ashamed of the gospel.
No doubt I am sold out,
Sanctified, water baptized,
Blessed and highly favored.
Lean over and tell your neighbor,
"I am not ashamed of the gospel."

Although my belief in the good news is on display,
There's one phrase I can't bring myself to say:
I give myself away so you can use me.[25]

Now, I'm happy to offer my time and money
For a good cause,
But what gives me pause
Is this concept of being a living sacrifice.
Because that means
I have to completely give up my life,
Which is the only thing in this world
I can truly lay claim to.
And since my days on this earth are few,
I've got things to do, people to see—
But what if what I want
Is not what God wants for me?
What if *that's* the most challenging way
He plans to use me?

Sadly, I'm only standing here after ample time spent
Unsuccessfully trying to circumvent God's plans.
At this very moment,
I'm fighting the urge to sit at a desk and write in anonymity.
Because spoken word's visibility
Presents the strangest form of vulnerability.
Every word I speak divulges a little more about me,
And I'm not comfortable with you viewing
The parts of me that you can't see.

Yet here I stand,
Feelings disclosed, soul exposed.
There's no hiding place behind the mic,
No escape route in sight—
Except through the Holy Spirit.

For when it appears,
It hides the imperfect beings that we are,
And Jesus Christ becomes the superstar,
Reminding us that a benefit of being used
Is in the power that is transfused
From Him
To those willing to decrease
That he might increase.
For just as Superman donned his cape,
God swoops down and makes us great
Whenever we find the nerve to say,
"I give myself away."

I think maybe our surrender to the power above
Is simply God's way of showing us how to love.
That despite all the crooks trying to steal hearts,[26]
Giving of yourself is still how love starts.
Though people polluted it, God has not diluted it.
What better way to show my love and loyalty
Than to dedicate my life to the one who gave His for me?
To declare that what I want is of no consequence.
In fact, His using me is the greatest compliment.
It's no coincidence
That being used puts us in God's presence.
I'm just thankful He wants me around,
Because I've found
That it's better to be used than to be ignored.
It hurts when the person you adore
Wants absolutely nothing from you.
I've been there before,
And I want more.
This time, I choose
To be used.

So I give myself away.
Because there is nothing else to give to someone who has it all.
Anything less than our everything
Would seem insignificant and small.
He gave all that He could give;
He died that we might live.
And each morning that we wake,
We should die for His sake.

Overdose
On the Holy Ghost
Until it's killed the pride, envy, and hate
That consumes us.
Then offer ourselves
That the resurrected Christ might live on through us,
Knowing that while this exchange might not be equal,
Our stories are His sequel.
And though you can never be as great as the original,
The point is not to dishonor His memory
And to bring His name just a little glory.

I'm grateful that God has cast me in this role.
I'm handing back over to Him creative control
And accepting that the most important line
He's given me to say
Is "I give myself away."

Birthing Your Dreams: Why Natural Labor is Best

One of my coworkers has a new addition to her family. A group of us oohed and ahhhed as she told us about the little bundle of joy.

Our excitement turned to confusion when she said that her mother and father were pulling overnight shifts to stay up with the newborn. While that might be normal for most babies, this situation was different. The "baby" we were discussing is a canine.

My coworker's parents own show dogs, so we would expect them to give their puppies additional care, but wasn't this over the top?

My coworker explained that the birth did not go as planned. Since the unborn pup was extremely large, the veterinarian recommended a C-section. That may not sound like a big deal, but it presented some post-labor complications. Because Mama Dog did not naturally birth Baby Dog, her maternal instincts failed to kick in. Since she did not recognize the puppy as her own, she did not nurse it. My coworker's parents were alternating shifts feeding the new puppy so that it would not starve. They were also watching to ensure Mama Dog, who felt no attachment to the pooch, did not eat her own child.

Hearing this story made me think of the dreams and desires we have for our lives. Though we may want them to materialize overnight with minimal effort, maybe there is a reason why many of us will need to birth them "naturally," grunting, sweating, and pushing the entire time: so we know what to do with them when they arrive.

If our birthing process was too easy—if dreams, jobs, and loves simply fell into our laps without us ever having worked or suffered for them—maybe we would be unable to care for them, ending up like my coworker's dog. In addition to the natural instincts we have to cultivate our dreams, we also need those learned in labor as we work toward goals we have yet to realize. The experience gained through our labor pains will give us the insight to properly nourish and grow the dream when it is eventually born. How devastating would it be to birth a dream after little or no hard work, and then starve it because you never learned how to care for it during the labor process?

Even worse than inadvertently starving your beautiful dream is the possibility of intentionally killing it. My coworker's parents were watching Mama Dog to ensure that she did not eat her pup. The baby that came *from* her was not safe *with* her because she had no attachment to it. Not only did she not recognize it, she resented it. Likewise, you and I can be a danger to things which we desire but never earn. We may not appreciate them and may resent the amount of work they require. Failing to recognize our dreams' beauty and promise, we who should nurture and protect them might be the very ones to bring them harm. How tragic.

It all boils down to trust. How much work is required on your end before God can trust you with the dream? See, I left out one minor detail about my coworker's parents and this new puppy: they bred their dog specifically to birth another show dog. So while Mama Dog had little attachment to her pup, all of their hopes and dreams for future dog shows were wrapped up in Baby Dog. Sadly, the vehicle they used to birth their dream was not emotionally invested.

God, in His infinite wisdom, prefers not to have a situation like that. Therefore, the Lord places the dreams in our hearts in the first place. He knows that without a passion for them, we will never care for the dreams that He plans to birth through us. While we have a desire for a dream at conception, the labor process helps us realize just how badly we want it. Once we have labored, He knows the dream is safe in our hands.

In our low moments, we might think that we are slaving away pursuing some dream because God has not favored us. We may think He has forgotten us. We may even think we are indefinitely put on hold because the Lord enjoys hearing us beg. We are mistaken.

God *has* favored you. He is not on some power trip by making you wait. And if He's like most parents, He does not at all enjoy listening to you whine. The truth is, He loves you too much to let you squander the blessing. The manifestation of your dream would benefit too many people for Him to allow you to kill it simply because you don't see its greater purpose. The one surefire way He has to ensure you respect, nurture, and use your dream appropriately is to hold your hand as you birth it the old-fashioned way—through much blood, sweat, and tears.

Finding My Forefathers' Faith

I don't know whether I found my forefathers' religion or if it found me.

Like in many families, it was passed down from generation to generation like banana pudding recipes and remedies for aching joints. Someone on my family tree decided to follow Jesus tens or hundreds of years ago. In time, like most beliefs, habits, and genes, the wonder-working power in His blood trickled down to me.

Someone once asked me why I decided to follow the religion of my parents. It made me think: how sure am I that I actually believe in Christ? Or do I follow Him for the same reasons that I've made *The Today Show* my morning news broadcast, choose Colgate over Crest, and take my grits salty rather than sweet: because my parents did?

Shortly after this question was posed, an old gospel classic came on the radio. It was Reverend Timothy Wright's 1990 hit "Who's on the Lord's Side." Listening to it in 2012 was like returning home—not to my parents' house, but to the beginning of my faith journey and, essentially, the start of my personal choice.

The interesting thing about that song (and the entire gospel's greatest hits record it was featured on) was that I knew every word by heart—not because my parents played it so much, but because I did. One of them clearly brought it into the house and likely played it from time to time, but I distinctly remember listening to it because it was what *I* wanted to hear, over and over again. Likewise, I also recall dropping new gospel cassette tapes onto the counter when it was my mom's turn to check out at Walmart, as well as attending my first concert, Kirk Franklin and the Family, at my own suggestion.

The significance of this has been more obvious to me during talks with friends who grew up in homes in which their parents only allowed gospel. That was not my experience. I freely listened to R&B, pop, and rap as well, but gospel was the only genre that actually made me feel something. I loved the beats and wordplay of secular music, and could even relate to some of the lyrics, but gospel was the only thing that produced a stirring in my spirit. I couldn't describe it, I didn't understand it, but I knew I felt it.

One might assume that my love for gospel was influenced by a childhood spent on church pews, but that was not the case. I don't have many church memories prior to middle school because that is the point when my family began attending regularly. I was not saved and baptized until I was 13 because my mother, knowing what it meant to inherit your family's religion, felt it was important for me and my siblings to make the decision on our own.

I vividly remember how I came to profess Jesus as my Lord and Savior. We had been regular church goers for a while. Each week when the preacher "opened the doors of the church," some force larger than me seemed to be pulling me toward the altar. But like a kid with a schoolyard crush, I never made a move. In hindsight, I now know that I did not have to wait for my immediate family to commit to a specific church in order for me to come to Jesus, but that seemed like the correct order of things in my young mind.

Imagine my surprise when I missed service one day and was informed that my family joined the church. I felt cheated. How could they join without me? I had felt this aching to be saved for a while and would now have to walk down the aisle on my own.

In hindsight, perhaps that's what was best for me. Maybe it needed to be a personal decision. Maybe God knew I had been holding out and did not want me using my family as a crutch, thus He orchestrated things so that I would still have to come to Him alone. God and my mother knew that while religious practices could be passed down the family line like high cheekbones, relationship had to be chosen of one's own free will.

Even in all my choosing, I recognize that simply being born into a Christian family significantly increased my chances of making Christ my choice. What if my family had been Muslim or Jewish? Would I still be a Christian today?

I cannot say with certainty what my religious beliefs would be had my upbringing not exposed me to Christianity. However, I can say with conviction that while my initial resolution to come to Jesus may have been influenced by my mother taking me to a Baptist church, my decision to choose Jesus repeatedly throughout my life was due to my own personal experiences.

There are occasionally some less-than-beneficial familial influences that you have to grow out of, but my family's faith was something I had to grow *into*. I had to have my steps toward college ordered so conveniently that an atheist would call it coincidence, while the provision accompanying it tied to the church in such a way that let me know it was God. I had to watch my difficult situations, and those of family members and friends, turned around with prayer. I had to have a few exhilarating moments in which I did something perfectly in what felt like an out-of-body experience in order to comprehend that it wasn't of my own strength. With each triumph, I was finding my forefathers' faith.

But more important, growing into my family's religion required some lost years in which I lost my grip on myself and my faith. I had to have some dark moments of solitude in which His was the only name I could call for help. I had to have sleepless nights with my face buried in a tear-stained pillow, the hour too late to call anyone and the situation too shameful to share.

In those moments, I turned to the only available presence. I felt Him in my heart, heard Him in my head, and breathed Him in the air. He beckoned me to His outstretched arms. I went from hyperventilation to still assurance in moments. Time and time again. He was with me when some didn't care to be and others simply didn't have the ability. He was my Savior not just in a centuries-old story I read in the Bible or heard preached from a pulpit; He was my Savior in every present day situation in which I needed saving, whether from the world or from myself.

That makes Him more than the God of my forefathers; it makes Him the God of my choosing.

Trust Fund

They called Him many names:
God, Jehovah, Jesus, Father—
But they all called Him good.

Whether they stood in pulpits,
Knelt at altars, sat in pews,
Or tread dusty roads and fields in flimsy shoes,
Their belief never faltered.
At times singing in soaring soprano or bottom baritone,
Whether in spirited shouts or mournful moans,
Sometimes in tongues that others could not understand,
Or even in silence, with just a slight wave of the hand,
In whatever manner they could,
They called Him good.

Because they knew...
He filled the hollow bellies of crying children
When the nation's headlines screamed depression;
Recession-proofed the family
So it never went without a roof overhead;
Kept the sons while at war so none returned as walking dead;
Spread offspring across acres of rich countryside,
Deed of sale in hand,
Faces brimming with pride
Because they came from slaves who once worked the land
For free.
They recalled how He
Kept danger—whether friend, foe, or complete stranger—at bay.
They'd proudly say He would never lead them astray
Because He'd ordered their footsteps,
Caught their every misstep.
So they called Him good,
Then ensured future generations understood
That it was He who hath made us and not we ourselves.

So I love to hear my grandfather delve
Into story, because he tells
How he went from tilling his parents' farm
To owning a business up north.
How he loved a sweet young woman who brought forth
A precious baby girl into this world.

How not long after, when his daughter was but an infant,
In anguish, he buried that wife.
But he cared for the child and left his heart to God,
Who finally sent another to share his life,
Which gives him confidence in the Lord's faithfulness and His plan,
Makes him sing with a perfectly odd mixture
Of dependence and strength
That he can't even walk without God holding his hand.[27]

And my granddad's just one of many,
As I've heard plenty of testimonies
From those close to me
About the goodness of God.
Those who think it not odd
That they integrated schools as children,
Then went on to earn Masters and PhDs;
Those who saw no irony
In being first-generation college graduates,
Only decades behind men and women whose only signature
Was a scribbled letter X;
Those who were not the least bit perplexed
As to how they overcame cancer or addiction;
Those who had the same conviction
Regarding how they raised fatherless children,
Or what greater power sent home wayward husbands and men.
No two stories were the same,
Each their own composition of exquisite joy and pain—
Yet the refrain remained the same:
God is good.

Now all I can do is pay forward that precious gift—
Lift my voice in song, poem, blog, or book;
Give someone on the outside an insider's look;
Offer the generations behind me a play by play
Of my life;
Portray every offensive and defensive move
The Lord has made along the way;
And pray, that in time,
They'll find the truth and spread the good news;
Hope that whatever name they call Him,
Whatever medium they choose,
They follow in their ancestors' shoes
And call Him good.

Mini-Me

I pray for my mini-mes –
The miniature versions of myself.
They're not the products of my womb,
Yet my dying hope blooms
By the light of their eyes.
So I baptize them in hugs, kisses,
Silent blessings, and verbal well wishes.
May they be better than me,
Let us pray for my mini-mes.

Today I prayed for my mini-me,
Right after she
Hugged me
When I most needed it.
Her spirit
Is soft like her plump cheek,
Her high-pitched voice
Speaks joy and innocence.
So I squeeze her tight,
Let my soul drink in her goodness,
Pray that when she gains
Pounds and inches,
Her insides remain just. like. this.
I want to spare her the pain
Of heartbreak.
So I make
A plea to God
To bury her heart in a capsule
With a note not to wake
Love before its time.
May no man be able to find it
Without first following the Word of God
Like a map to its burial spot,
Where he'll drop to his knees,
Digging through dirt with bare hands
To reach her treasure.
May his intentions be measured
By his endurance.
Mini-me,
I pray God preserve all about you
That is precious.

Yesterday, I prayed for my mini-me.
This one is on the precipice of puberty,
At that age when she pulls away
Though I beckon her nearer.
I caught her scowling
At her reflection in the mirror,
Eyes slinging darts at imperfections.
Uncomfortable
With the skin she's in.
I guess it's begun to sink in —
That some designer declared
Her hips too wide,
Legs too big,
Butt too round —
And even if she'd managed to ignore that,
She hasn't yet drowned out the sound
Of the world chiming in.
Thus it begins:
The tendency to despise self,
The desire to look like someone else.
I want her to see the beauty in her curves,
Want to will her the nerve
To love a unique physique,
Hope she'll be deaf to her peers' insults.
I pray, Mini-Me,
That you'll learn early
What some haven't mastered as adults:
To love yourself unconditionally.

The world is praying for my teenage mini-me.
It's a spiritual melody
Marked by a cacophony
Of languages and dialects
As different nationalities erect
Mutual hope
Before varied gods, saints, and statues —
A chorus of support for a girl who refused
To be silenced.
I feel a sense of pride for her —
Malala* —
Less than half my age and Pakistani.
Yet like me.

We both write,
Blog to express ourselves
And make the wrongs right.
But she is better than me,
For my own need for approval
Is my censor,
Yet she voices an unpopular opinion
Even in the face of terror.
She used words to advocate
For her right to be both educated and female,
To be bold rather than frail,
Free rather than political hostage.
After being gunned down
By men seeking to muzzle her message,
I exhaled when she left the hospital,
Having won the fight for her life.
Mini-Me,
I pray they have not succeeded
In dimming your light.

Pray for our mini-mes—
These miniature versions of ourselves.
They are not the products of our wombs,
But our dying hope can bloom
By the light of their eyes.
So baptize them in hugs, kisses,
Silent blessings, and verbal well wishes.
May they be better than you and me.
Let us pray
For our mini-mes.

Note: On October 9, 2012, Malala Yousafzai, a 15-year-old female student and blogger, was shot in the head on her school bus by members of the Taliban because of her campaign for girls' rights to attend school.[28]

Little Man

We prayed for you.
When your tiny body was still curled
Into a ball pressing on your mother's navel,
Before you were able
To lay eyes on this world
Or it upon you,
We who already loved you
Interlocked fingers, intertwined spirits, and bowed our heads
Over every path your feet would tread
And every door you'd one day walk through;
We prayed the universe would be kind to you.

Little Man, I prayed for you when you arrived,
That my feeble hope for this world might be revived
Through you.
For I'd be remiss
If I didn't learn from the ease of your smile,
If I missed
The point of God making your laughter contagious,
If I failed to realize the simplest
Way to experience Him is through a child.
So, I prayed
That I'd be less likely to downplay miracles
Once I'd seen them again through your wide eyes.
That I'd find the sweetest version of peace by singing hymnals
As your lullabies.

Now as you tear through this world
In adventurous leaps and bounds,
Little Man,
I pray that the world will be your playground.
That the wondrous places you desire to go
Will not lie behind "Do Not Enter" signs.
But in the event that they do,
That you will be undaunted,
That you'll never consign
Your destiny to any power outside of you.
And while you're in the discovery zone,
I pray that the most valuable thing you find
Is the real you.

Hope you'll be unwavering in the pursuit of your truth,
That you'll let no one define it for you.
I pray that you find your wings,
That God-given greatness deep inside;
That you don't spend a lifetime
Crawling when you were born to fly.
And I've prayed
That He'd have legions of angels on standby—
Your own private protective detail.
I pray that they never fail,
That you don't share the fate of Trayvon Martin
Or Emmett Till*,
And still
Countless other young men
Convicted to death
By an unlawful citizen court
Because of their dark skin.

I pray, too,
That your brother will indeed be your keeper,
That you never incur
The wrath of some other
Young black man's self-contempt.
I pray that he'll neither succeed
Nor attempt
To take your life because he's believed
This country's longest living lie:
That people have less value
When they come in a darker hue.
I pray that you never feel
The fear that capsizes a black man's heart
At the sight of unjustified blue-and-white flashing lights
In the rearview.
I pray that you never learn how traffic stops
Can morph into brutal attacks,
That your precious face
Never slams against harsh pavement,
That you never feel an oppressor's boot upon your back,
That life never finds you bent
Over
From carrying the weight
Of the world's hate.

I pray that you never see the inside of cell blocks,
That grace and mercy flock
To you
As if the prayers and blessings
Of generations of saints
Have been stored up in your name.
I pray not that you find fortune or fame,
But that purpose pursues you—doggedly—
So that you're never tempted to
Settle for someone else's aspirational hand-me-downs.
I pray that you realize joy is found
When you refuse to recycle
Society's used goals.
I pray that your soul will help your mind to see
That the best dreams come outside the REM cycle
Of sleep.

I pray that when you're older,
You'll find a beautiful woman
Who inspires you to be a better man;
That you'll have the good sense
To ask for her hand
And stand
Before God,
Promising
To be gentle with her heart,
To nurture her confidence,
To never provoke her insecurity.
That together
You'll raise strong, brown boys and girls,
And that one day,
Your beautiful family
Will take over these prayers for me.

Until then,
Little Man,
I'll be praying.

Note: Emmett Till was kidnapped and lynched in Money, Mississippi, on August 28, 1955, as retaliation for allegedly whistling at a white woman.[29]

In Response to Psychology Today

This poem was written in response to "Why Black Women are Less Physically Attractive than Other Women," an article that appeared in Psychology Today *in May 2011. The article was later removed from the publication's web site.*

There I was, minding my own.
Well, really,
I was scanning social media on my phone.
So technically, I was minding mine
And whichever parts of people's lives
They chose to share,
Trying to block out the many ways
That life has a tendency be unfair
To brown girls.
Only to find the icing on the pity party cake
A good ten times in my timelines.
Breaking news:
The entire world was yet again minding mine,
Dousing fuel on the journalistic fire
That's predetermined me to a lifetime of singledom.
Just when I chose to ignore all societal clues
That Mr. Right doesn't come
For African American women,
Psychology Today announced
That of a random sample of men, most agreed,
That of all women, the least attractive,
And presumably the last with whom they'd want to be,
Was someone black like me.

And I was honestly surprised
Because, although we're consistently criticized,
I forget that the world views us
Through distorted eyes.
That, despite all indications
It needs corrective lenses,
It continues to squint
As it pretends
It has 20/20 vision
When neither its mind nor eyes
Are open enough to realize
That oftentimes,

Preference is just a matter of what you're most exposed to
And that the Creator was too creative
To confine beauty to a single hue.
Perhaps He gave people too much credit
When He hoped they'd be able to tell
That there's something especially sweet
About skin that can range from vanilla to caramel
To milk chocolate to Hershey's Special Dark.
Maybe He's a genius whose uncultured audience
Just can't appreciate His art.
And the All-Knowing knew all too well
That it would be this way;
But the gifted don't dumb down their work
To appease those viewing the display.
So God followed His heart
And made woman in an array of beautiful shapes and colors.
And foreseeing her struggle,
He gave the brown girl thicker skin than the others.
So while she knew she'd never be some men's first choice
Because she was different than the norm,
She was content with the love of her Creator
And the one from whose rib she was formed.

But there comes a point
When even the most reserved woman is compelled to make a sound,
And even the most humble
Eventually tire of fading into the background.
So she crashed the great American dream,
Spray painting its white picket fence because it seemed
To need a little color.
And even more to the homeowner's chagrin,
She walked through the *front* door, on a mission,
Head held high—
A far cry from the woman once beat into submission.
Standing with brown hands on capacious hips,
A smile tugging at her full lips,
Once downcast gaze now staring observers right in the eye,
With a steady voice she proclaimed:
"I have arrived."

And as she worked the room, the men couldn't help but watch her move.
But they claimed they were only hypnotized by her backside.

And while it had been known to leave men speechless,
Pride and prejudice would not allow them to confess
Their fascination with the way her eyes resembled opaque black marbles
With flickers of light where the hope shined in.
And they failed to mention
Their intrigue as she spoke on subjects from healthcare to education,
And they wondered
How she mastered acclimation without succumbing to assimilation.
For she was all up in their classrooms and boardrooms,
Head of class and head of state,
Managing stocks, bonds, and estates
With Afros, locs, cornrows, relaxers and micros—
Any hairstyle she chose.
No-nonsense professional
Juxtaposed
With around-the-way girl,
Waking up each morning determined to take on the world
Regardless of the horrors of the night before,
No matter who pounded down
Or walked out her door,
She keeps shining,
Striving,
Thriving
As men try to figure out why
They can't help but turn their heads for a peek as she walks by.
And other women spend a fortune and a lifetime under the knife,
Injecting lips and gluteus maximus in an attempt to look like
The least attractive woman men ever did see.

But Tameka, Monique, Ebony,
If it's any consolation,
All I ever wanted to be was one of thee.
So if I were to travel back to the moment before my conception
And sit suspended in time and possibility far above the sun,
Bouncing on my Heavenly Father's knee,
And I was free
To choose the circumstances of my birth and my life on earth,
Even knowing at times I'd catch some flack,
I'd tell him:
"Go 'head, show off, hold nothing back.
Just please, God,
Color me black."

A Woman's Worth

"A wife of noble character who can find? She is worth far more than rubies." ~ Proverbs 31:10 NIV

A woman who does not know her worth will sell herself short every time.

I was selling myself short one day (in my thinking more so than in my doing) when I came across this text. I wanted a romantic relationship, but nothing was happening. I was asking God why.

I was familiar with Proverbs 31, but for the first time, I wondered why rubies were used to describe the value of a wife of noble character. As far as I could tell, rubies were not very popular, particularly in modern society. So what made a ruby so special?

I took to the Internet to learn more. What I discovered made me appreciate the value of rubies, and therefore the value of women, all the more.

According to the International Colored Gem Association (ICA), in the "world of gemstones, the ruby is the undisputed ruler." Ratnaraj, the name given the ruby in the ancient language of Sanskrit, means "king of precious stones." It is the jewel of royalty, often included in the insignia of many royal families.

Who knew the ruby had such clout? And a wife of noble character is worth *far more* than rubies? If we take a closer look at the jewel, we'll notice some other interesting characteristics that also apply to the wife of noble character:

They are rare. A ruby is considered a corundum gem. There are similar gems that are also classified as corundum , but a ruby is set apart by its color. In order to be distinguished as a ruby, the corundum must be red; any other corundum of any other color is just a sapphire.

Rubies are even rarer because, due to environmental conditions, many of them crack during growth. Very few are able to grow to a significant size and crystallize to form perfect gemstones. Therefore, a ruby of more than 3 carats in size is a rare commodity.

Life, and the growth that accompanies it, can change a woman—and not always for the better. Jay-Z told us "once a good girl's gone bad, she's gone forever."[30] That may be extreme, but the point is that a woman who maintains noble character after growing in an environment as harsh as Single America is a rare find.

They are valuable. We all know the economics of supply and demand, so it should come as no surprise that given their rarity, rubies command top dollar. In fact, because of the limited number of large rubies, they often cost more than flawless diamonds of the same size.

It is interesting that our society is fascinated with diamonds. One might assume that this makes the ruby less valuable, but not so. We hype up diamonds because they are marketed to us. Some of us can't even distinguish between a diamond and a cubic zirconia. However, a jewelry expert knows scarcity determines value. A good man knows a woman of character's value and believes she, as the ruby, stands out among colorless diamonds.

They sell themselves, but not really. Technically, a ruby can sell itself, meaning its value is such that little advertising or gimmicks are required. However, the ruby does not literally sell itself. There are brokers for that. A broker negotiates with buyers to determine an acceptable price based on the ruby's appraised value. The ruby is not involved in the discussion.

There are numerous women stressed out from the constant task of self-promotion. However, marketing herself is not a woman's responsibility. She need only maintain her status and value as a ruby. The buyer can tell at first sight that a ruby is something special. He observes and, if interested, approaches the broker. The jeweler runs down the stats and names a price.

It is important to note two things: 1) a woman does not "sell" herself in the sense of bartering or chasing down potential buyers, but she does realize the need to put her best foot forward; and 2) the "price" for a woman of noble character is about so much more than money. A man's finances may have some bearing on whether he can "afford" a woman of noble character, but the Heavenly Jeweler also takes into consideration *his* character, his ambition, his patience, his holiness, etc.

When the price is placed on the table, only serious buyers stick around. They'll either make the purchase on the spot or do what's necessary to scrape together enough money to acquire this gem that caught their eye. Non-serious buyers who realize the item is not going on sale, or those who cannot afford the ruby, exit.

Women often assume that there is something wrong with them when a man does not pursue them. Perhaps she meets a guy at an event and they seem to hit it off, but he doesn't ask for her number. Maybe she regularly interacts with a man who is obviously attracted to her but has not made an official move. If he seems impressed by the ruby, why isn't he buying?

Who knows? Seriously. Who knows? But does that have to mean something is wrong with the ruby? Maybe the man is not in the market for a ruby. Maybe, like me, he's clueless about jewels and has no idea how precious a ruby is. Maybe red's not his color so he prefers diamonds. Maybe he already has a ruby in the jewelry box and is not into collecting. Maybe he simply cannot afford the ruby and never will. Maybe he and the Jeweler on High are in the midst of a negotiation. Maybe he's not about substance and thinks a cubic zirconia will meet his needs just fine. Maybe he's only window shopping until pay day. Maybe he doesn't even like jewelry. The list goes on and on. There are numerous factors, independent of the ruby's worth, which might keep a buyer away.

A ruby is valuable because of what it is, not who owns it or is considering buying it. It would maintain its value even if it sat in a jeweler's case for its entire lifetime. Women have a tendency to tie their value to whether or not they have a man. However, the ruby is proof that worth is independent of the buyer (or lack thereof).

A wife of noble character is worth more than rubies. Ladies, know your worth and expect to be treated accordingly. There is no sampling the merchandise. There are no clearance deals. Put your heart in the hands of the High Jeweler. He will weed out potential buyers, ensuring that they are serious, ready, and able to care for you.

A Woman's Worth 2: The Self-Appraisal

In the "jewelry store" of love, a wife of noble character is worth far more than rubies. It is natural for a woman to jump from that statement to the presumption that a man will pay top dollar to make her his wife. However, while all women are valuable, we fail to realize the full intent of the Bible's comparison if ladies don't pause to honestly ask themselves: do I belong in the ruby section?

Proverbs 31 does not say that any woman is more valuable than rubies. It specifically refers to a "virtuous woman," or a "wife of noble character." Dictionary.com uses various phrases to define virtue and noble character: possessing moral excellence; righteous; chaste; of good reputation. These characteristics are equivalent to the red color of the ruby: they are what set the woman apart.

And that's only the definition. In its description of a virtuous woman, Proverbs 31 describes a superwoman. Since I grew up singing "I'm *not* your superwoman"[31] along with Karyn White, this is a tough pill to swallow. I won't list each of her wondrous works, but I'll point out a few indicators of a wife of noble character's awesomeness.

She knows how to treat a man.

The Bible says "the heart of her husband doth safely trust in her." Not only can her hubby trust her with his money, children, and business affairs, he can trust her with his heart. Men guard their hearts more closely than women. They need to know they have entrusted their heart (their hopes, dreams, insecurities, and secrets) to a virtuous woman.

She knows how to treat others.

The virtuous woman speaks to others "kindly" and with "wisdom." She is not quick to give others a piece of her mind every time something does not go her way. She understands the power of words and uses them to enlighten and encourage. The woman described in Proverbs 31 also helps the poor and needy. She is naturally a giver, always thinking of helping others. She is not a taker or someone who uses others for her own gain.

She brings him respect from others.

"Her husband is respected at the city gate." The respect a man receives is not solely a result of his own actions. It is influenced by the woman on his arm. While President Barack Obama's résumé is on point, First Lady Michelle, with her own impressive résumé and beauty, makes him better. Conversely, the wrong woman can cause people to lose respect for a man. I won't point fingers, but I'm sure you can name a quality male celebrity who chose a questionable woman—and you never looked at him the same.

I'll assume that any woman who even *thinks* she might be a ruby is not obviously questionable. Yet can she maintain her virtue throughout the marriage? A good woman gone bad, perhaps one who sneaks around behind her husband's back or behaves embarrassingly in public, reflects negatively on him as well. A virtuous woman's presence should increase (or at least maintain) the respect that others have for her man.

She knows how to raise a family.

A woman of noble character's household is in order. She adds the finishing touches that make a house a home. Additionally, "the bread of idleness (gossip, discontent, and self-pity) she will not eat." Though busy, this woman is content and does not feel sorry for herself. A lady sets the household's mood; as the saying goes, "If mama's happy, everyone's happy." Yes, the husband should do what he can to keep the wife happy, but she has to work with a brother. Being consistently picky, critical, and unsatisfied makes a woman less than virtuous.

"She got her own."

Read the full passage if you want to know her many side hustles, but the point is this: a virtuous woman has things going for *her*. She has purpose outside of her wifely duties. They can be non-paying hobbies or paying jobs, but they are hers. A woman should not lose herself while caring for others. She definitely sacrifices for her family, but the virtuous woman realizes that having a life of her own is essential.

Proverbs 31 concludes on this note: "Many women do noble things, but you surpass them all." Anyone can be noble for a day or season, but the woman worth more than rubies does not do noble things on occasion. Virtuous is who she is—it is her character and the condition of her heart.

One of my favorite Anthony Hamilton songs is "Her Heart." In it, he confesses mistakes he has made and the fact that he has, figuratively speaking, run away from his woman. The important part is the chorus, in which he sings, "But her heart won't let me lose her. No matter how I try, I just can't say goodbye and lose her."

We can discuss looks, education, money, and other factors, but Anthony says her heart is what touched his heart. It's what made him stay, the one thing that made him want to be a better man. And the Bible backs him on that. The passage says "charm is deceptive and beauty is fleeting, but a woman that feareth the Lord shall be praised."

For all the women intimidated by this description of a seemingly perfect woman, I'll share something else about rubies to relieve your concern: the red color is their most important feature. According to Gem Brokers, "inclusions [internal flaws] do not impair the quality of a ruby unless they decrease the transparency.... On the contrary: inclusions ... could be said to be its 'fingerprint', a statement of its individuality and ... proof of its genuineness and natural origin."

Virtuous does not mean you are perfect. However, a person of noble character corrects her mistakes. She takes advantage of the second chance that God has given us all and makes every attempt to live with high morals. She understands that every day is another chance to get it right.

Imperfections make you who you are and verify your authenticity. If you've been polished by the High Jeweler and are still transparent (or as one definition says, still "made visible by light shining through"), you are still a ruby. My interpretation: if people can consistently see the light of God shining through you, your imperfections do not detract from your value.

Ladies, make sure that your character and your heart are right. A good man will consent to pay a high price for you because he'll know that those things do not depreciate it with time; they are what make you worth it.

Note: The descriptions of the virtuous woman are taken from Proverbs 31: 10-31. Four different translations of the Bible were used.

The God in Me

On more than one occasion,
I've been told there's just *something* about me.
Something you can't quite put your finger on,
Yet even the blind can see.
It's more than a twinkle in my eye
Or the warmth of my smile
That makes even those in a rush want to pause…
And stay a while.
It goes beyond confidence
And outshines poise and grace.
It's evident whether I'm in sweats
Or a ball gown with a made-up face.
It transcends physical beauty
And is the source of my inner glow.
It's the reason I appear cool and steady
Even when storm winds blow.
Something that makes some love me
And others hate me at first sight.
It's more than the rhymes and words I write in the poems I recite.
It will remain whether my bank account should shrink or grow.
It's not the degrees I have or even the people I know.
"What is it?" some might ask, and still others look on in dismay.
No, I don't have a big ego like Kanye and Beyoncé.[32]
Maya Angelou was close,
But it's not just that I'm a woman, phenomenally.[33]
I think it was more aptly put by Mary Mary:
It's the God in me.[34]

It is the curious case of Christianity—
Strange to many, but the true definition of free.
Sin had me bound, but God removed the restraints
And enabled me to be me with no constraints.
The God in me cleared the cobwebs from my idle feet
And challenged me to not live life from a spectator's seat.
He gave me dreams and aspirations,
Accompanied by the hope that they would come true.
Now I'm running trying to make 100
Because 99 ½ won't do.[35]
And when my footsteps lag and I feel less than inspired,
He reenergizes me
So I don't feel no ways tired.[36]

The God in me persuaded me to join the Lord's army
And be all I can be.
He makes me judge myself not by human standards
But by what He asks of me.
Is my body a temple, presented as a living sacrifice?
Or a playground
For whomever says sweet words and treats me nice?
Do I rejoice in the blessings of others
Though my breakthrough may be pending?
Do I keep the faith during tough times,
Trusting that He will write my happy ending?
Is life all about me,
With no thought to the trials of my fellow man?
Or am I sharing God with others
Through kindness and the deeds of my hand?
Do I fear the murderous plots of enemies
And shrink from the sting of insults hurled?
Or do I know that greater is He that is within me
Than he that is in the world?
And some have said that hell hath no fury
Like that of a woman scorned;
But though I've been hurt by friends and lost loves have I mourned,
The God in me softens my heart which was once hardened
And says earth should have no joy like that of one pardoned.

You ask how, even when my world may be collapsing around me,
Can I still give Him praise?
It's because hymns are crescendoing in my soul
Telling me trouble don't last always.
Psalms and scriptures are dancing a two-step in my head,
Reminding me of the blood which,
For my soul, Christ once shed.
That and the blood now running warm through my veins
Is all the proof I need that He reigns.

What gives me the audacity to hope and the nerve to believe
That whatever I ask in His name I just might receive?
The God in me, who's able to shatter glass ceilings,
To fight diseases that doctors have no way of healing,
To open doors that society has slammed in my face,
And to reform what elitists may consider as my place.
He is my personal shield when I take refuge in him.
He is the bright light in a world that is otherwise dim.

It is the *perfect* God in me that balances out my imperfection,
The *loving* God in me that shows His other children affection,
The *pure* God in me that purges my uncleanness,
The *mighty* God in me that strengthens my weakness.
And while many people profess many gods,
That which is at work in me
Trumps all others.
He is the one, the only, the Holy Trinity:
The Father,
Providing my needs
And protecting me from dangers seen and unseen.
The Son,
My Savior and High Priest, who,
On my behalf, continues to intervene,
And the Holy Spirit,
Interceding for me with groans that words cannot express.
The three conjoin within me
To create an anointing that I cannot suppress.

And what makes this all the more remarkable
Is that I'm a far cry from who I was long ago.
There were countless things I didn't like about myself
And even more that I didn't know.
But it's the God in me
That makes me secure in who I'm called to be.
Now, don't take this the wrong way,
But in that respect, you should get like me.
Then, when people ask for explanations
On the inevitable change in you
And the things that you do,
Just make sure you give credit where it's due
And proudly say it's the God in you.

The Evolution of Love

I fell in love on a Sunday.
Heart racing, knees shaking,
Heavy tear-brimmed eyes, and stomach full of butterflies;
Hard-pressed to unleash feelings formerly suppressed,
I made the life-long trek from pew to altar and professed:
"Jesus, I love you."

And I loved Him with a child-like adoration.
But it's hard to maintain that initial elation in the face of temptation.
He was all in, ready to carry me over the threshold.
But my love was puppy love, so I put *our* love on hold.
We became something like friends with benefits;
I told him, "I'll spend time when my schedule permits,
Call you when I need you, but I just can't commit
To anything more than an occasional spiritual hit."

Then somewhere along life's way, things got complicated.
I was educated but unmotivated,
Sophisticated yet invalidated,
Unfulfilled in the life that I had created,
And painfully aware that romantic love is overrated.

So I came running back, bewildered and broken.
And when the preacher's final words had been spoken,
I wondered if God could forgive all the things I'd done wrong.
Then the organ wailed and He whispered, "They're playing our song."

I fell, instantly settling into His embrace,
Became that clingy chick with no respect for personal space.
We were joined at the hip, or actually my hip to his pierced side,
And we grew closer with each stride.
He had me up so high—
I was the typical blushing bride.

Yet at some point, the honeymoon ended.
I got comfortable and left our love unattended.
I was preoccupied with people I befriended
And hustles and hobbies that left me overextended.
So we began to talk less and less,
Because we'd grown so close that I felt like He could just guess.
Though He could, I was hurting myself with the emotions I suppressed.

Then there was the matter of the disappointment.
I tried to accept that I was better off without dreams
To which He did not consent,
And that one day there would be some great return on my investment.
But the longer I feigned contentment,
The more I succumbed to resentment.

See, we were still together yet drifting further and further apart.
And the rift between us had created this gaping hole in my heart.
Because the only thing worse than *not* being with the person you love
Is being with them knowing all the things your relationship is void of.
So I was with Him, but I missed Him.
Because though I never had the courage to utter the words to His face,
I told myself, in the back of my mind, maybe I just needed some space.
And while I didn't have a new boo,
I had a feeling that my distance made me untrue.
And I knew, deep down in my core,
That He had always loved me more,
And that my lack of trust was the root of most of the pain that I bore.

But then,
As grace would have it, it was Sunday.
The mood was so similar to the previous times I'd fallen
And I could no longer harden my heart as I heard Him calling.
So as the choir sang, God pulled at my heart strings,
And I put my hand back in the hand of my King.

I've fallen again, completely head over heels,
But now not just because of how it feels;
This time for His character and the simple fact that He's always been there.
And I love Him knowing that sometimes life will seem completely unfair,
That there will be highs and lows, triumphs and woes,
But that pain is the only way anything grows.
I'm willing to fall in love with Him over and over, as many times as it takes
Because I finally get that life without Him puts my soul and sanity at stake.

Lord, I'm determined to let nothing stand in our way.
But if, by chance, my foolish heart should stray,
Please help me to recall
That Sunday when I first began to fall.
Remind me of all that we've been through,
And I promise to find my way back to you.

Terrifyingly Beautiful II

There's this guy.
And he is terrifyingly beautiful.
With him, I feel both at home
And terribly uncomfortable.

See, we're kind of doing this awkward dance.
I prance in front of him
Every chance I get,
And just when he starts to advance,
I change my stance—
Become the wallflower,
Desperately hoping he'll find the nerve to make a move
And that magically,
Our bodies will instantly settle into a familiar groove.

Luckily, because he's so much braver than me,
He does, and we do.
Until the thoughts in my mind become louder
Than the melodies we're dancing to.
Then I question the moves I'm making,
Wonder if he can feel my hands shaking.
My fear?
That the magic will end and the real me will appear.
And since I have no idea how long the music will play,
Like Cinderella at the stroke of midnight,
I run away.

Because he's terrifyingly beautiful.
And if I were to stay,
I just might fall dangerously in love.
Not that pretty love Beyoncé sang of,
But the kind that makes you lose all common sense.
That chameleon type of love,
Changing my eyes from brown to green
At the slightest hint of another woman on the scene,
Expanding my world well past black and white
And beyond shades of gray;
The lines will be so blurred into a rainbow of colors
That I'll choose to stay
Well after the writing's on the wall,
Still clinging to the long-gone euphoria of the fall.

That hangover love,
Buzz faded, crashing down to reality,
Heaving up the toxic remnants
Of something once guzzled with carefree glee.
That self-destructive love,
Chugging poison in typical Romeo and Juliet fashion,
Brimming with enough passion
To make grim,
Irrevocable decisions
On a childlike whim,
Hastily plunging knife into chest
At the thought of life without him.
That insane love—
I'm having visions of strait jackets and padded white walls,
Entangled in one-sided mental brawls that feel inescapable,
Doing things of which I never thought myself capable.
Schizophrenic love,
Stumbling back and forth
Across that thin line between love and hate.
My mind is screaming:
"Kiss this terrifying beauty goodbye
Before it's too late."

But when he reaches out for me,
My heart refuses to say no.
As fearful as I am
That love might be an impossible feat,
There is a glimmer of hope
That won't allow me to leave.
So we dance,
Sometimes as perfect partners,
And when I'm thinking too much,
Like a pair with four left feet.
But that's just when I hear a voice
Interrupting the DJ's beats,
Like that of a parent
Thundering over the loudspeaker at a middle school dance.
Only it's God—and I'm like Adam in the garden,
Unable to meet His glance,
Afraid to seek His face
As He bids me from my hiding place.
And as I clutch leaves
To conceal my heart's natural beauty,

This time the question He asks is:
"Who told you, you couldn't love like me?
More heart,
Less head;
Keeping no record of things said,
Wrongs committed
Or compliments omitted;
Giving more than you receive;
Cleaving when it would be easier to leave;
Loving with patience and kindness.
Who told you
You had to repress
The parts of you
That I like best?
Perfect love casts out fear,[37]
So it and I can't both live here.
Forget the imperfect examples
You've seen in the past;
True love conquers and heals—
It lasts."

Then I know what I have to do.
Because this man is
More beautiful
Than terrifying,
And I'd hate myself for not trying.
Hope maketh not ashamed;
So though past loves left my heart maimed,
I proclaim
That this could be all I ever hoped it would be,
The very thing I feared I would never see.

I close my eyes,
Throw caution to the wind.
And pray that this beautiful terror
Is a Godsend.

I Want to Hold Your Hand

Did I ever tell you about the time I let the stranger hold my hand?

As *Golden Girls* riot Sophia Petrillo would say, "Picture it: Washington, D.C., 200X."

It was a beautiful summer night. My girls and I had been keeping vigil inside a dead nightclub in hopes that the scene would find its pulse again. But ready to call it, I pulled the plug, chucked the deuces, and rolled out solo.

It was late, but since I was in a good part of town and the streets were sprinkled with other party goers and deserters, I felt safe. I took my time strolling to my car, thankful to breathe in air that was not first filtered through a roomful of lungs. And just as I adjusted to no longer feeling the club's stereo system vibrating in my chest, something else set my heart racing.

It was a hand. Masculine. And swiftly, expertly enveloping my own. Its owner had snuck up behind me, taken my hand, and matched my stride before I even noticed him. I turned toward this crazy man, prepared to reclaim my hand and reprimand him for invading my personal space.

But I didn't. He was smiling, a gorgeous grin that made you forget why you were angry in the first place. His eyes were soft, but they boldly dared me to pull away.

Now, I usually reserve public displays of affection, especially prolonged PDA, for men that I particularly like—or at least know. But here was this strange man holding my hand, and here I was, letting him. Though I've had no problem pulling my hand away from men I've actually dated, I was comfortable and content to stroll hand in hand for blocks with this beautiful stranger.

Handsomeness aside, there was something about this man's grasp that kept me holding on. His grip was firm but not threatening, disarming yet strong, comforting and confident. It said, "I'm not letting you go, but I won't stop you if you want to break free." It was perfect.

Recently, I recalled that brief walk holding hands with a stranger. The trigger was a Kelly Price song. Though it was three minutes long, I decided that the lyrics' last seven words, about holding hands, were the most important part.

It's a gospel tune, one in which the songwriter confesses a list of unknowns, specifically what tomorrow will bring. But that's okay, she sings, because "I know Who holds the future, and I know Who holds my hand." The first part of that sentence is usually enough to help me sleep at night. But that conjunction? Maybe it's my current station in life, but the second part of that statement seals the deal.

I've held hands with a few men in my day. I've even loved a couple. But I have a million other memories with them that overpower those spent simply holding hands. Therefore, it was this brief encounter with the stranger who *only* held my hand, and perfectly at that, which reminded me how much weight that can carry if done properly, and if appreciated sufficiently.

The perfect hand-hold demands nothing but vulnerability and gives a world of strength, peace, and comfort in return. It guides rather than tugs. It is a reminder of someone's presence, and a promise that you don't have to walk alone. It gives you courage to venture places you ordinarily would not. It is a steady grip when your steps falter. It gives you the freedom to let go, but the encouragement to hold on. It is perfect.

So many of us focus only on the fact that God holds the future. We look to Him for clues of what the next day will bring while steadily laying a heap of problems at His feet. However, maybe God wants us to value the fact that He holds our hand as much as we appreciate the fact that He holds our tomorrow.

Perhaps what God wants most from us is vulnerability, and enough trust in Him, to let Him hold our hand. Even when we haven't known Him very long. No matter who's watching. Regardless of where He leads us. Maybe He beams each time we choose not to pull away.

There are so many places God wants to take us and so many miracles He wants to perform. Yet sometimes, He approaches us like that handsome stranger did me, only offering a hand to hold. Something so simple that, He hopes we'll come to realize, is so incredibly powerful.

I Want Jesus to Walk with Me

I want Jesus to walk with me.[38]
Like he walked with those who came before me—
Slaves hunched over tobacco, cotton, and sugar cane;
Like he guided those brave enough to make their own train
Aboard the Underground Railroad to obtain freedom;
Like he stood with soldiers of glory against Confederate slave masters;
Like he ran with freedmen fleeing the South when their former captors
Picked up torches and crosses while hiding behind white hoods;
Like he walked with them when the North didn't make good
On its promise of liberation.
When, like them,
I come to the realization
That I'm still not free,
I want Jesus to walk with me.

Harriet Tubman said she could have led a thousand more slaves
To freedom—
"Had they known they were slaves."
Imagine going to your grave
Not discerning that you don't control what you do
Because bondage was the only life that you knew.
Tricked into believing you didn't have a right to want more.
Or imagine me, reading Tubman's quote countless times before,
Until one day God flicked on a light switch in my brain
And it became painfully clear that my soul was in chains.
But I couldn't really explain how it got that way,
Just that something began with "one time"
And transitioned to "always,"
Until I could no longer raise my hands in praise.

I wondered: how could I break free?
Martin Luther King, Jr., said,
"Freedom is never voluntarily given by the oppressor,
But must be demanded by the oppressed."
So I need Jesus to walk with me
Like he walked with my ancestors in protest.
When I can find no honor in my hometown,
When I've been cast aside and beaten down,
Turning peaceful walks into Bloody Sundays,
When I've been shot in Mississippi driveways.

I want Jesus to walk with me
Like he walked with my ancestors in protest—
Give me the courage to cause unrest
To the social order of the one who seeks to control me.
Help me to stop pleading on bended knee
And stand and demand what belongs to me.
I want Jesus to walk with me
As I command mountains to move and demons to flee,
As I declare some things in life not dead, but asleep.
Like Peter, I want Jesus to walk me across the deep.
And when necessary,
I want him to part some impassible Red Seas.
Walk with me
When I can't manage to watch and pray in my Gethsemanes,
When I deny him three times before the rooster crows,
When I doubt and boldly ask him to disclose who He is
When the truth is: He's shown me time and time again.
When I can't see right, I need him to touch my eyes and restore my sight.
Walk with me when I'm in the desert 40 days and 40 nights.
When I'm weary in well doing and most open to the devil's wooing,
When I'm a prodigal daughter who can't find my way home,
Jesus, walk with me, talk with me, and tell me I am your own.[39]

And I won't be demanding—
Just being in your presence is enough.
So I'll quietly crawl to touch the hem of your garment
On those days when I can't keep up,
Knowing that one day I'll mount up on wings as an eagle and fly.
Jesus, lead the way when I can't see through the tears in my eyes.
Be with me when I try to lift my hand in worship
But feel like it's nailed to an old rugged cross.
When the devil's grip insists that God has finally lost,
Jesus, help me to realize
That if, each day, for you, I die,
One day, with you, I'll rise.

My forefathers endured too much for me to live in bondage.
My Savior endured too much for me to live in bondage.
I pay homage each time I ask Jesus to walk with me.
For where His feet tread, the captives are set free.

Morning

Morning

The sun has kissed the darkness goodbye.
I smile as its rays tickle my face.
My eyes shine with newfound hope and resilience.
Encouraged by the promise of an expected end
And motivated by the epiphany
That You only want what's best for me,
I realize that answers will come
At established points along the journey.
So I quicken my pace,
Confident in a destiny
Shaped by Your hands.
With each step I take,
I cast shadows of my former self
On the ground behind me.
I am as new as this dawning day.
Eternally grateful,
I celebrate daylight's triumph over night.
I marvel
At a sun that has never shone so bright.

Faith for Surprise Endings

I noticed something as I was reading a novel once: I don't read the titles of chapters. I ignore those short, carefully crafted phrases (that would take me all of two seconds to read) because I'm the type of reader who prefers not to have any hint of what is coming next. I realized then that I *read* for surprise endings. However, as I considered my faith, I wondered why I don't *live* for them.

Apparently, some readers view novels differently than I do. I gasped when a friend told me she skips to the end of a book to learn its conclusion, then goes back and finishes the story. Come again? It never occurred to me to do such a thing. But come to find out, she's not the only one! Many people practice this backwards style of reading.

I'm baffled by those who sneak peeks at endings because a book is about so much more than its outcome. It's about the characters, their quirks and interests, their attributes and flaws. I want to know them personally before I know what happens to them. I want to grow to love or hate them with each sentence that I read. I want to be totally vested so that I'm just as shocked or relieved as they are when we reach the story's conclusion. I want to experience the journey that is the book more than I want to know the ending.

Some of the same people who read a book's ending before its middle would never skip to the final scenes of a movie and then backtrack to view it in its entirety. What's the difference? I think it may have to do with the length of the body of work. It takes even a speed reader several hours to complete a novel, but a movie usually wraps up in two. Is the suspense of a book simply too great to wait for it to develop naturally? And if we can't spend several hours in suspense when it comes to fictional characters' lives, how can we possibly wait weeks, months, and even years for the biggest moments of our own lives to unfold?

We can wait if we view life as I view fiction. We can bear the agony of not knowing if we want to experience the journey of life more than we want to know how it ends. If we allow ourselves to become engrossed in the daily joys and hurts, the scenery of our surroundings, the strange characters we encounter, the great men and women who hold our hearts, we'll realize that a story is always more interesting and more important than its conclusion.

Waiting is possible when you have faith in the Author, that He will make it a good read packed with interesting story lines and colorful characters. You can wait when you look at the Author's collective body of work and realize that every single book has been a page turner. You can wait when you accept that you're actually not waiting at all but that you're an active participant in your life story and that you're meant to laugh and cry as each moment happens. You can wait when you acknowledge that, like every great book, when you reach your life's last scene, you'll find yourself disappointed that it has come to an end.

Consider your life. Now stop trying to guess the ending. It's already written. Just enjoy your story.

Finding Your Own Way

I get antsy when God does not answer my prayers. My mind fidgets as my restless spirit repeats the same questions: Why? How? When?

As time passes, I flip through the Bible hoping some major revelation will jump off the pages. I pray fervently, sure that if I was just a little more persistent, God might suddenly make everything crystal clear.

Eventually, if I still am unsure, I become desperate. I search for meaning in every little thing I come across: the books I'm reading, the blogs I peruse, the timelines of my social media accounts, the people in my life, and every song or sermon that drifts into my ears.

Though answers can come in those mediums, I have noticed that many times they do not. I have also come to understand that this does not mean God is ignoring my prayers. The problem is that I want an instant reply or an immediate fix to my problem when the things that I wrestle with the most are things that God wants to reveal to me over time.

We live in a society in which we are so terrified of making a mistake that we refuse to take a step if there is no guarantee on how the situation will unfold. I have sat in church discussion groups listening to people practically beg preachers to tell them what to do in some area of their personal lives. I have scrolled hundreds of questions submitted to motivational speakers and life coaches, all soliciting advice for every simple and complex life situation. And I have spied countless people reading self-help books that claim to be able to help with every problem and condition under the sun. We want answers, and we want them now!

What we fail to realize is that while God guides us through life using the Holy Spirit and the Word, and although He has placed people in our lives who are capable of giving wise counsel, sometimes He intends for experience to be our teacher. Other times, God does not plan to give us the Cliff Notes of the life story He is writing for us. He'll give us enough direction to get through the present, but may not choose to share exactly what we can expect in the future.

God requires that we trust Him, whether He gives us all the answers or leaves some things as a mystery. We should walk by faith rather than by sight, whether an entire path is visible or only a few steps. We should believe that the Lord is good to those who diligently seek Him and rewards those who place their trust in Him. We should believe that if we are in relationship with Him, God will make plain that which we need to know at the time in which we need to know it. We should trust that if we should fall or make a mistake, God is gracious and merciful enough to pick us up and turn us in the right direction.

There is an old hymn that says, "We will understand it better by and by." Many of the things we do not understand today, and many of the trials we have faced, will be made clear to us in time. Sometimes we will not understand it on this side of Heaven. However, in most situations, I truly believe that God will reveal information to us bit by bit on a need-to-know basis. No one can map our paths for us. But with His guidance, we will each find our own way. And when we look back, so much more will make sense.

Lady Wisdom

While she does not play hard to get,
Wisdom is far from easy.
After all, she is a lady.

Many have tried to woo her
With charming words and sweet nothings;
They fall on deaf ears.
She is unmoved
By the cunning courters
Who have asked her hand
With wrong intentions.
She respects not
Those who make lackluster bids for her affections;
She turns her fair cheek from their calloused lips.

Wisdom desires to be earnestly sought.
She is weary and leery of casual suitors
Who attempt large withdrawals
Following tiny deposits.
Their funds are insufficient,
Their only investment
Being the clichéd wine and dine.
They forget she is a lady
Who casts not her pearls before swine;
Patience is her greatest virtue,
So she must be pursued over time.

Lady Wisdom,
When courted properly,
Doles out her pearls one by one:
A little knowledge for this situation,
A little discernment for that occasion.
Just enough to keep one coming back,
To make the noncommittal vested.
And when she is finally respected,
When she feels valued
And knows her advice has found a keen ear,
She gives herself fully,
Wrapping her lover in an intimate embrace,
Sharing her instruction indiscriminately

Until, at last,
Her steadfast pursuer,
Clutching a full strand of her pearls at his chest,
Stands draped in all her splendid glory.

I do not claim to have won her heart,
But because she respects my diligence,
Lady Wisdom humors me.
And the more I talk to God,
The more she opens herself to me.
So still I chase
In hopes that one day she finds me worthy.
And in the meantime,
She drops a pearl here,
Offers another there.
And I retrieve them,
String them together with my own words—
And share.

Reinventing Yourself in Life and Love

"I just want people to see me the way you see me."

I don't recall telling him exactly *how* I saw him, but as the Rude Boys once sang, maybe it was written all over my face.

Our meeting was by chance, our goodbye an act of fate. He hailed from some far-off city and was in D.C. temporarily. I was here indefinitely, surviving without thriving, anxious for the next big thing. We were opposites attracting yet had similar enough interests to avoid awkward pauses as we talked. And from the moment our lives collided one chilly night in Chinatown, we were each other's interim.

Since temporary lives stop somewhere short of forever, we did as well. However, in some future conversation as we ran through the topics typical of two whose journey together has come to an end—the good times shared, our present time apart, and the fact that our lives were not destined to merge again—he said those words: "I just want people to see me the way you see me."

I wondered: had he only shown me the parts of himself that he wanted me to see, or had he introduced me to the person he hoped to one day become?

I think it was a combination of the two.

Many of us have an internal struggle between who we presently are—which is a direct result of the events, decisions, and people of our past—and the better person we are striving to become. This battle between our actual and preferred selves is the root of many of our problems and breeds much of our unhappiness.

It makes sense that being here with me allowed him to easily be someone he liked and admired. The fastest way to reinvent oneself is through relocation. At some point in my own life, I dreamed of doing the same: heading to some distant land where I would shun rigid Corporate America.

The Sheryl I saw in those fantasies used words to paint vivid pictures by day and painted the town red by night. That Sheryl was also a flirt who carried only a backpack full of issues rather than a couple of suitcases. She was uninhibited, balking at others' expectations and standards. She was free.

But for some reason, it felt like I had to abandon life as I knew it in order to download Sheryl 2.0.

We do ourselves a disservice when we assume we have to find someplace else to be our best self. Packing up and leaving is harder than it sounds. Just ask him.

But who says you can't be who you want to be, right where you are? There may be things that people have come to expect from us, but if they are contrary to our desires for ourselves, who says we can't let them go? There may be aspects of our personality that we keep in the shadows because others may not approve, but how much happier might we be if we let those sides come out to play in the lives we have already built? There may be demons in our past—but suppose we are trying to outrun what should be confronted?

Perhaps we have created situations that are not easily escaped, but maybe we could find freedom if we approached it like a prison break, planning meticulously until we saw our chance. We may be in relationships in which we want our special someone to see us the way they did in the beginning: untainted by confusion, hurt, and the complexities of life. Maybe the key to returning as close to that place as possible lies in our willingness to give them that version of ourselves all over again.

Say that you could immediately walk away from your present life. What would you take and what would you leave? What does life look like in your utopia? How are you spending your time, and with whom are you sharing it?

Every day is your chance to become the person of your dreams, one step at a time. So what's stopping you?

Mirror, Mirror

Mirror, mirror on the wall,
I'd rather not stand before you at all.
There is no fair lady in your looking glass.
In stark contrast
To the woman I expect to see,
I am met instead by a child—
One whose wild eyes make silent pleas
For approval,
Constantly seeking affirmation
That she is beautiful.
She is repeatedly denied it
By the only being
Who has ever made her beg for affection,
The only person obsessed with her imperfections.
But still, to her abuser she remains loyal.
Quietly, selflessly dutiful.
Despite her innocence,
Years of practice
Has her
Standing, beautifully flawed,
Before this mirror as if it were a firing squad—
Chin up, shoulders squared
Taking shots for the whimpering woman
Who never dared
To step out front.

Mirror, mirror on the wall,
This woman I'm becoming still stalls
At the sight of you,
Transfixed by all those things
She's been brainwashed to believe must be fixed.
But she's finally learning to push through.
She stands before you
For as long as it takes to find her power.
She no longer cowers
Behind the little girl inside.
Instead she steps up to the child's side,
Grabs her trembling hand,
Kneels down to her level
And revels
In all that is right.

She shines light on all the beauty
She was once so quick to dismiss
Because she never looked away from the faults
Long enough to notice.

Mirror, mirror on the wall.
I barely recognize this woman at all.
I am changing—
Gradually, but drastically.
She and the little girl have melded into one,
A single pair of curious eyes
Watching as the world's handiwork is undone.
Mirror, when I stand before you these days,
I am unable to look away.
It is like lying on an operating table
Undergoing open heart surgery
As my spirit hovers in the air above my body,
Taking it all in.
It is a fascinating transformation,
My entire being under construction.
I am watching my heart, beautiful and bloody,
Beating steadily in the palm of the doctor's hand.
He is calm,
Humming quietly
As He gently wipes the organ clean,
Removing years of muck and mire
Until it gleams
Like new.
He smiles at His progress,
Beams with pride,
Then proceeds to caress
My hardened organ
Until it is putty in His hand—
Soft and squishy as he originally planned.
I watch as he shapes it, meticulously,
Until my heart is the perfect clone of His own.
He squeezes it, then releases,
Squeezes and releases again and again
Until it slowly eases
Into His rhythm.
When we finally share one heartbeat,
He nods approvingly—
The transplant is complete.

Mirror, mirror on the wall,
I'm starting to resemble the Greatest One of All.
I must say, my journey has been worthwhile
Because anytime your glass surface is within my view,
I can sense His smile
And instinctively take His cue.
I stand before you,
Grinning broadly at this woman who
Is oddly familiar,
Like an old friend,
Who knows the places you've been,
All your weaknesses and flaws,
Yet because of the memories you share,
Handles them with care.
I am staring into eyes that have seen evil
Up close yet still twinkle
With the light of His holy presence.
I see a woman whose very essence
Is defined by One who is the quintessence
Of perfection.
So she can quit chasing it
And start basing her value
On being a reflection
Of Him.
And it's like the strangest case of déjà vu
Because this is who
I was created to be.
Mirror, mirror,
What a wonderful change;
I'm becoming the real me.

I Found My Everything—In You?

"I found my everything in you."

That Mary J. Blige lyric, featured in a song of the same name, ranks up there with *Jerry Maguire*'s "You complete me" as one of the most swoon-worthy phrases one could say to a significant other—but should not. It is romantic and flattering. It is what many of us have dreamt of hearing since we read our first fairytale or were introduced to romantic comedies. But is it a wise, or even realistic, expectation?

I once wrote a blog post about our tendency to fear love and marriage because of previous heartbreak and relatively high divorce rates. When a reader posted my piece on Facebook, I got into an interesting conversation with one of her male friends. He said, "I would love to be married but can't imagine how I can be successful meeting most, if not all, of the daily needs of someone else…. That level of accountability is uncomfortable for me."

He explained that in his past relationships, he had fallen short of the man that his woman needed him to be. He possessed several attributes that most ladies want in a man—hardworking, taking care of traditionally "manly" household chores, good credit, etc. However, among the ladies' complaints about him (in my words): lack of sensitivity, inflexibility, not being romantic enough, and being too possessive.

Since I can respect a man who not only takes his responsibility as a husband seriously but also tries to do everything in his power to keep his woman happy, I wanted to let this issue marinate in my brain and my heart.

So with my thoughts now well-seasoned, I cooked up this piece because, although the afore-mentioned song is one of my favorite MJB tunes, unfortunately it is indicative of the problematic views we have about love and marriage.

My unsolicited take?

We shouldn't expect to find someone who is everything we want. Our culture prefers to acquire things ready-made. No assembly required, no additional parts needed, no fuss, no wait, no problems. This is fine for products, but not for people. What are the chances that someone with a

159

different personality, upbringing, and life experience will be everything that you want and need in a mate the moment you lock eyes? Slim. But maybe they can grow into being as close as possible and vice versa. Perhaps it is more realistic to find someone who meets the major criteria that you know you cannot live without, and then jointly commit to growing together in order to love the other as he or she desires.

No person should be your everything. Everything? That means without you, I have and am nothing. That means that you, a human being capable of changing and making mistakes, are solely responsible for my happiness. Truthfully, I don't even want to be my own everything. I let myself down, I'm indecisive, I keep bringing up old stuff…. As a human, I'm incapable of meeting the standard. But I know a divine being who can. In his song "Everything," Tye Tribbett encourages us to set our sights higher as he sings to God: "You're everything to me."

Ego won't allow you to be less than someone's everything. Ego says "This is who I am; take it or leave it." While I fully support the essence of the "take me as I am" mantra, we all must admit that we could be better. No matter how great we believe ourselves to be, there are some aspects of our personalities and our lovin' that can be improved. A man may have to practice a little more emotional intelligence than usual to be with me, but perhaps that will make him more kind-hearted and better able to relate to others. Conversely, sometimes I am, ahem, overly emotional. Maybe the future Mister will help me take fewer things to heart.

If we're not so defensive about the areas in which we fall short, if we don't expect the other person to simply deal with it and instead are willing to take the time and energy to improve, maybe we can have healthier relationships. Is it easy? No. But if you're not ready to be challenged, you're not ready to love.

We should be looking to other people for some things. While I've mentioned that you risk being disappointed when you expect someone to be your everything, let's also consider that serving as your everything is an overwhelming responsibility for your significant other. I'd dare say it's a burden. When you constantly tell someone how he doesn't measure up, he feels inadequate. Plus, I can't help but wonder whether the measuring stick we use is always fair.

I remember a time when I really wanted to do something that I was sure no one in my regular crew would also be interested in doing. I was temporarily blown—until I thought of another friend outside of that circle. We're good friends but just don't have as many opportunities to hang out. I hit her up and she was immediately down to go. It was wrong for me to be disappointed my regular group of friends would not want to attend this event. Though we enjoy many of the same things, it's unfair for me to expect them to like *everything* that I like. That's why I have other friends.

Though there are clearly some things you will need your boo to do with you or certain conversations you need to feel comfortable having with him, and while this does not get anyone off the hook for developing certain attributes as a person, I wonder if there are times we could take the pressure off of certain people in our lives simply by occasionally turning to others. This is not an invitation to cozy up to other members of the opposite sex. It is simply a suggestion to take advantage of all the beautiful relationships and friendships you've already been blessed with, particularly the same sex ones, rather than consistently draining the primary one.

I would be lying if I said I didn't want to be everything my future hubby has ever desired in a woman. But since I'm working on having more realistic expectations, the most I can hope for is coming pretty close to the woman of his dreams—and then committing to spend a lifetime trying to close the gap. I pray he'll do the same.

For the Lovers

Love is…
An electric smile whose currents shock your heart into submission.
A slow dance under a star-filled sky, with the crickets providing the music.
A private joke shared in one knowing glance across a crowded room.
A stolen moment in the middle of a busy day.

Love is…
A strong hand resting gently on the small of your back; it calms your
tattered nerves.
A haven for your hopes and dreams, a vault for your faults and nightmares.
A prayer that begins with their needs and ends with your own.
A perpetual chance to give and forgive.
A vow.

Yet one of the most blatant tricks of the enemy,
One of society's greatest conspiracies,
Was convincing us that this is all that love can be.

Love is…
A child rushing into your arms
And holding on tight.
A laugh so deep that your tummy and cheeks ache.
A favorite meal prepared by familiar hands.
A soothing voice when the world is shouting demands.
The hype man who won't let you wail
"It's my party and I'll cry if I want to."

Love is…
A listening ear.
The tears another sheds with you.
A place of rest after a trying work week.
A look that peers through the eyes into the soul.
The feelings that don't fade.
A cool downpour on a sweltering summer day.
A warm embrace in your coldest winter.
A hand clutching yours when sunny days fade to black.
An affirmation when you need to hear it.
The words you don't have to say.
The chance to simply *be*
Without explanation.

Love is family, friends, and BFFs.
Love is the kindness of a stranger.
Love is an outstretched, nail-scarred hand.
Love is a sermon that speaks directly to you.
Love is a song that speaks *for* you.
Love is a simple "I'm thinking of you."

Love is that thing many spend a lifetime
Desperately seeking
Without realizing
It is all around them—
And that it even dwells within.

Seasoned Love

I didn't see this coming.
Was trudging through life, mind set
Solely on surviving,
And it snuck up on me.
A couple decades and hundreds of miles
From the place where we met,
I sat in a pew with tears streaming down my face,
Heart swelling in chest,
At just the thought of you.

My mind was grasping at straws,
Trying to understand
How time could possibly draw
You more beautiful.
How the once black-and-white picture I had of you
Could suddenly shine bright
With tints of yellow, blue, and purple.
And each time I taste your rainbow,
The unthinkable occurs:
I, a girl obsessed with subjects, nouns, and verbs,
Am at a loss for words.

I can't pinpoint how or when
I fell more deeply in love with you.
Maybe at midnight in a dark room,
Doomed to the prison of my thoughts.
And while I dare not downplay
Freedom papers signed in your blood,
At this point in life I love you most
For being the peace I desperately sought.
For, after having fought
All day to hold it together,
Having acquiesced to society's request
That I turn my frown upside down,
When the day's end finally found us alone,
I loved you more
For giving me permission to break down.

Or maybe it was your chivalry,
As each moment of this journey
Has been trekked with you as cavalier,

Serving on the front lines
As I bring up the rear.
You have been both guide and shield,
And I have come to realize
That each time you offered me a place to hide
From vultures and the elements,
That with each new path you revealed
And every glint of hope,
You gradually coaxed me to lay down my pride.
So now my every footstep, every heartbeat, every thought,
Yields
To you.

My fate is sealed:
You are my heart's first choice.
My soul is sensitive to your touch,
My raging mind lulls to a hush
At the sweet sound of your voice.
You are the crutch
My hobbling spirit rests its weight upon,
And I am too far gone to protest.
Heart on a platter, standing vulnerable
Before your holy gates,
Yet warmed by your grace shining upon me,
Basking in the glow of my soul mate.
There is no shiny, princess-cut stone
Symbolizing our love,
But you are the rock of my salvation,
And our procreation
Begets words that bring hope and liberation
To the multitude.
In your presence,
Creativity leaps in my womb.
So if writing is the call you've given,
I'll comply out of obedience and gratitude
Because there's nothing more scary
In this big, bad world
Than the thought of disappointing you.

And I know that to love you properly,
I must trust you with my destiny.
So I take a front row seat in your life class,

Determined to pass
This new form of math
In which,
Regardless the troubles that cross my path,
I count it all joy.
Because I understand
That in the most complex algorithms of life,
You are always greater than.
More than the situation, the hurt, the pain—
Yet no greater
Than you were before.
Nothing new, same you—
But now I see you up close.
And there are no blemishes,
No imperfections,
Just countless dimensions
Of your love that I've uncovered.
Finally discovered
That you have always been the missing piece,
Able to fill any void,
A chameleon
Easily transforming
Into whatever I need you to be.
Lord, I love you
For all that you've been to me.

Terrifyingly Beautiful III

I have never imagined a world in which you did not exist.
Long before I had my first kiss,
Before I wrote rhymes that gushed over a first crush,
I knelt in front of a pink-and-white dream house
With a Barbie in one hand
And a dapper man named Ken in the other.
And when my little mind pieced their lives together,
There was always a child to complete the fairytale.
So I knew that one day,
I, too, would wear a white gown and veil,
And soon after, welcome you.
My childhood self was also no stranger
To life-sized dolls, which I wrapped in swaddling clothes,
Then laid in make-shift cribs that may as well have been mangers,
Because I think I may
Have subconsciously knelt at your altar
Each day in play.

I have been thinking of you
Now, consciously and consistently,
Feeling as if you are overdue.
For I have been pregnant with your possibility for decades,
And the biological reality that you cannot be indefinitely delayed
Leaves me feeling betrayed by time.
I used to join other little girls in song:
"First comes love, then comes marriage,
Then comes the baby in the baby carriage."
But who knows
If love can even tell time?
What if it takes too long, or marriage is a no-show?
What, then, becomes of you?
Do I stand firm with faith that whatever's meant to be will be?
Or do I stage a spiritual coup,
Join the masses of women planning for contingencies
By consulting doctors to fill the void of potential daddies?
It has not come to that, and prayerfully never will.
Yet and still,
I've been thinking.

Contemplating, but not praying,
That small distinction perhaps conveying

That I still believe deep down that you are my destiny.
And that quiet knowing is perhaps the greatest fear gripping me.
That you, in all your splendid glory,
Will need more than I have to give,
That I might not live up to my own standard of motherhood,
That I could possibly only be "good"
At a position that requires greatness,
Be mediocre for the one person desperately dependent upon my excellence.
I don't want to cut corners where you are concerned.
I think you will have earned my unwavering dedication
Simply by blessing me with your presence.
Hence, this lifelong aspiration steeped in trepidation.
Anticipation dueling with reservation,
A struggle between my lifetime of desire and the present knowledge
Of what you will require.
I'm scared
That you may never come.
And horrified that when you do, I won't be prepared.

Yet even in the midst of all that fear,
I can't imagine not having you here.
Perhaps one day, when the time is just right,
This temporary confusion will have been worthwhile.
I will delight in the pure beauty of your smile,
I will cherish the way you fit into the crook of my arm,
I will carve out a nook in my heart reserved solely for you,
I will wonder how you wear the best parts of me better than I do.
All apprehension will be erased,
Replaced by contentment
From the fulfillment of our destiny.

Terrifyingly beautiful little one,
Overwhelmingly gorgeous daughter or son
With my plump cheeks and your father's smoldering eyes,
It pains me to admit this fear that defies explanation.
But I told myself I ought to,
On the off chance that you
Should inherit your mother's obsession with perfection.
In case you have a seemingly unreasonable fear of all that's beautiful,
Or an unhealthy tendency to shun the very things that make you special,
I want you to know that Mommy had them first
And that the best way to overcome any fear is to jump headfirst
Into that wondrous ocean of endless possibility.

I want you to have our relationship as an example of the attainability
Of dreams that both thrill and intimidate.
I want you to know that the presence of fear does not negate
The evidence of purpose.
So as I consider that which awaits us—
A powerfully precious,
Terrifyingly beautiful love—
I am reminded that every good and perfect gift comes from above,[40]
And that His strength is made perfect in my weakness.[41]
So if I should ever be blessed to meet you face to face,
I have assurance
That by His grace,
I will be all that you need me to be.
And in all my flawed beauty,
You will know me
Simply,
Sweetly,
Intimately,
As Mommy.

There's No Such Thing as "Too Good to be True"

One day, I had a strong feeling that good things were on the horizon. I saw endless possibilities. I suspected that maybe dreams do come true. And I cried.

They were not happy tears, but rather tears of anxiety and bewilderment. But why would the potential for especially good times provoke such emotions? Because beneath the hope, I can't help but wonder: what if, traipsing through the desert of life, I am staring thirstily at a glistening expanse of water in the distance—and it's not real? What if what I think I see is actually a mirage? What if it's all just too good to be true?

After I dried my eyes and God calmed my spirit, I wondered what skeptic-turned-hater coined the phrase "too good to be true." Who decided there was a threshold for good and that anything beyond that was simply a myth?

"Too good to be true" is a fallacy upon which many have built the invalid argument that "this is as good as it gets." Those who have been bamboozled into that way of thinking do not know just how amazing "good" can be.

Here's the good news:

God gives good gifts. "Every good and perfect gift is from above, coming down from the Father." *(James 1:17, NIV)* If it's good, it's from God; if it's perfect, it's from God. Therefore, our prayer should not be for good and perfect things because the Word says those are prerequisites for any gifts that come from Him. Instead, we should ask God for the wisdom to recognize His gifts, and then the courage to reach for them when they are within our grasp.

God _wants_ to give us good gifts. Psalm 84:11 says "The Lord will give grace and glory; no good thing will He withhold from those who walk uprightly." God is not trying to keep the good stuff from you. If you are walking with Him and the "thing" in question is good, He is not going to withhold it. However, we should not be so quick to call everything good because…

God's definition of good is better than ours. In Genesis, when God created heaven and earth, He said "'Let there be light,' and there was light. [Then] God saw that the light was good." The same was true when He separated land from sea; when the land produced vegetation; after He made the sun, moon, and stars; and when He made animals and mankind—He saw that it was good.

If *I* created the entire world and its inhabitants (which are all so beautiful and intricate that mankind is still trying to figure them out), I would have declared it all awesome. I might have even said that it was spectacular or mind-boggling. Yet the Bible says God simply saw that it was good.

Unlike humans, God does not speak in hyperbole. He does not exaggerate His works, power, or character. He declared all the things He made in the beginning "good" so that *He* would set the threshold for good. He wanted us to know that when He said the world was good, when He said the sea and land were good, it was the same good as the gifts He has promised us and the same good as the things He will not withhold from us. He wanted us to know that nothing is too good to be true.

Are you walking in the desert like me? Do you see water, either a few feet away or even way off in the distance? You probably don't want to get your hopes up. However, with all the good things that you know, why wouldn't you walk over to the see if it's real?

Lightning Bugs and Love: It's All in the Chase

When temperatures drop, signaling the shift from summer to fall, many singles employ creative methods to find temporary snuggle buddies. However, for those looking for "the one," I think we can learn some lessons from a summer pastime many of us remember fondly from our youth.

Here are a few pointers I picked up chasing lightning bugs (aka fireflies) that just might be the secret to landing love:

Look for the light. The easiest way to spot a firefly is when it is illuminated. Interestingly, lightning bugs light up to attract mates. Their glow is an indication that they are ready and willing. In love, sometimes we assume that because someone is flying solo, we can catch them. Negative. Look for someone who is not only single, but also lit up, showing all the signs of someone who wants to be caught. They are easiest to identify and to pursue.

You can't really chase it. When you chased lightning bugs as a child, you saw a flash of light and took off running, right? But the more you chased, the more it eluded you. Dizzy and winded, you finally collapsed in the grass empty-handed. Then, after catching your breath, you were more strategic. You realized you should stand still and just watch it. After a while, you were able to anticipate where it was going. And as you slowly made your way in that direction, it flew right to you. Love is the same way. If you chase it doggedly, you will run around until you're exhausted with nothing to show for it. Yet if you watch it closely, then time your move, it will come to you.

What you're chasing is rare. While writing this, I realized that I have not seen a lightning bug in a long time. I wanted to ensure I remembered them correctly, so I did some quick research. I learned that firefly populations have decreased over the years. Unfortunately, true love is rare these days as well. Be patient as you wait for it to light up your night's sky. Then when it does, make your move.

Have a plan for after you catch it. So, you've captured it. Now what? Sometimes you chase something so long that you don't give much thought to what you will do with it once you have it. Many of us are anxious for love, but have no idea how to *be* in the relationship once it arrives—giving, supportive, faithful, etc. It's not good enough just to boast that you've caught it.

If you have no use for it, let it go. Most people put captured lightning bugs in a jar. However, the insects can only survive there for a day or two. Once that time has elapsed, the kind thing to do is to set them free. However, some people let the lightning bugs die a slow death, or worse, crush them. While love can obviously survive more than a couple days, sometimes we can guess when it is not going to last a lifetime. If you care about the person, let them go before you crush their spirit.

True maturity means that your efforts to find love have evolved like those of a child chasing lightning bugs. You began innocent, hopeful, and foolish. Then, as anxiety and frustration set in, you ran in circles desperately trying to get your hands on that which eluded you. Finally, you found the peace that rests with the wise person who waits patiently for it to drift toward them. At which stage of love are you ?

1 Corinthians 13

"If I speak in the tongues of men or of angels, but do not have love, I am only a resounding gong or a clanging cymbal. If I have the gift of prophecy and can fathom all mysteries and all knowledge, and if I have a faith that can move mountains, but do not have love, I am nothing." ~ 1 Corinthians 13: 1-2 NIV

Love,
Teach me your language.
Decode your sighs,
Illustrate your passions,
Interpret your moans.
Disclose your terms of endearment,
Acquaint me with your terminology of tenderness.
Show me how to kiss in your native tongue.

Love,
Direct me through your melodies that I might learn to play them by ear.
Recite your chants and prayers until I commit them to memory,
Lead me in your cheers and rallying cries,
Drill my eardrums on the rhythm of your heartbeat,
Spell out your wisdom in closed captioning
For those days when the world is too loud.
Sketch your commands on the tablets of my soul,
Tattoo your promises on my heart.

Love,
Show me your ways.
Paint me a color wheel naming every one of your moods,
Make a manual with explanations for each of your smiles,
Demonstrate the synchronous strength and submission of your embrace.
Confess the cadence of hope in your hellos,
Instruct me in the stressed syllables of your goodbyes.

Love,
Give me a cautionary glimpse of your curse words and offenses,
Lest I utter them unintentionally.
Make me a detector of your enemies' lies.

Replace my self-absorbed singular pronouns of I and me
With the inclusive plurals you have mastered: us, our, we.
Teach me your tenses—the impeccable present,
Which recognizes that far more than the future is perfect.
Introduce me to your senses—
Touches that heal inflamed wounds,
Sight that detects hurt behind the stormy anger in a lover's eyes,
Ears that glean affection amid incoherent mumbling.
Dumb down the jargon some have used to complicate you,
Delete the flamboyance
Until all that remains is the simplicity of your beauty.

Love,
Help me to adopt your dialect of trust.
Teach me to tell time on your grandfather clock of patience,
Educate me in your colloquialisms of compassion and clemency
Until I've learned to exonerate even the culpable.
Help me adopt the vernacular of the vulnerable,
Inform my fashion sense until I proudly sport my heart on my sleeve.
Empower me to speak in absolutes and infinities,
Remove the conditions I have for evoking your presence.

Love,
Spill your secrets upon the floor of my soul.
Articulate your wishes,
Teach my tongue sweet words to contrast the salt of your tears.
Confide your disappointments, even if the blame rests with me.
Annunciate your whines,
Help my blinded eyes recognize your white flag of surrender.
Teach me the significance of your silence,
Guide my fingers across the Braille-like goosebumps
Dotting a virgin lover's skin,
Confide the insecurity behind your stutter,
Admit the uncertainty behind your stammer,
Disclose which infractions make your heart a closed fist.
Quiz me until I'm fluent in vocabulary that affirms
And chases the bad thoughts away.

Beautiful, mystical love,
Pardon my ignorance,
Forgive my arrogance.
Abide with me,
That I might
Teach another
Who teaches others—
Until the whole world
Sounds,
Touches,
Sees
Like you.

The Scenic Route
(A Wedding Poem)

Perhaps you wish you'd gotten here before now.
That somehow,
God allowed your paths to cross many years before;
That maybe this journey could have been less of a chore
Had He saved you the bore
Of dull dates with ones not destined to be your soul mate.
Sometimes we wish He'd saved us the emotional expense
Of time invested in those not equipped to go the distance.
But as you recount the twists, turns, yields, and dead ends,
Remember that it was all to bring you to an expected end.

Maybe God meant
For each of your past journeys to land both of you
On the same road at the same moment.
So every second before you laid eyes on one another
Was well spent
Because it steadied your minds
And prepared your hearts,
One for the other,
And cleared your eyes
So you would recognize each other.

True love takes the scenic route.
It is more concerned with arriving at its destination intact
Than it is with speed.
It pauses to smell the roses and to see the sights before it proceeds.
It heeds warning signs, moving with care.
It's gracious enough to share
The road,
Selfless enough to help its partner carry the load.
Sometimes the way is uphill, the night dark, the terrain rough;
But with God, with each other, you will always have enough.

Because you let patience have its perfect work,
Here we are,
The past now seeming so far
Behind.
In a moment designed
By God with the same care He gave
When He numbered each star in the sky.

And as you fly high
Together on the wings of His love, enjoy the view.
Know that few
Ever reach such heights,
So thank God for the ride.
And then as the excitement subsides,
And you find yourself back in the real world
With the rest of us,
Trust
God to still lead you across these ordinary trails.
Trust
That a union with Him at the head never fails.
And on those tough, uphill days
In which every part of you would much rather coast,
Dig deep,
Knowing your love will boast
The time and trials
That builds legacies,
That lives on through triumphs and tragedies,
That counts its miles
In laughter, tears, and smiles,
That after decades,
Still stands tall
Because you declared today
That you were in it for the long haul.

I pray
That your journey has more progress than setback.
But even then, may you never lack
Faith, wisdom, and love.
And above all else,
May you make God and each other
Your primary pursuit.
Congratulations
And take the scenic route.

My Love Story: The Remix

I usually memorize lyrics fairly quickly. If I love the song, I'll play it so often that my brain will embed the words into its cranium. For those songs that I am fond of but don't necessarily feel butterflies for, I listen often enough that I can at least commit their choruses to memory. However, despite the fact that Faith Evans' song *Tears of Joy* captivated me the moment I first heard it, I have had quite the challenge reciting its simple lyrics.

In the song, Faith sings that after all the tears she has shed due to the heartbreak of previous relationships:

"I'm crying now, but it's not like before.
Baby, these are tears of joy.
Ain't been the same since you walked through my door.
Baby, these are tears of joy."

I was immediately taken by the song because it made me realize that, at least romantically speaking, I have never cried tears of joy. My tears have resembled Faith's tears of old: an ugly emotional side effect of hurt, the involuntary leakage of a bleeding heart. But tears brought on by joyous occasions and the beauty of love? That was a foreign concept to me.

I decided that, having cried enough sorrowful tears, happy tears sounded like something to which I should aspire. I looked forward to the day that a man would help me make the transition. In the meantime, I'd just sing the song.

Except I couldn't. I made attempts, but I always messed up the lyrics. I would join Faith in singing, "Baby, these are tears of joy." However, when I reached the line "Ain't been the same since you walked through my door," to my horror, I found myself singing "Ain't been the same since you walked *out* my door." Over and over.

As one who adores ballads, there is no doubt in my mind that I have loved many a song about heartbreak. I'm sure a vast majority of my singer "sheroes" have sung countless songs about men walking out on them. Therefore, the words might roll so easily off my tongue due, in part, to the musical influences throughout my lifetime.

However, if I'm honest with myself, there is a more personal explanation for my inability to get the words of Faith's song right. It traces back to the very reason I find the tune so appealing in the first place. Maybe I'm accidentally singing the wrong lyrics because those particular words echo my experience. Perhaps a part of me thinks that men walk away, rather than stay, because in my love life, they have done just that.

Of course I know that all men don't leave. I have seen repeated examples of men who stay and love their women unconditionally. Therefore, I am openly optimistic and have told the world repeatedly that I still believe in the power of love. However, deep down in my heart, apparently I still have doubts. Clearly my previous unhappy endings, as well as my tendency to listen to the same sad love song, have me singing a different tune than the one which I claim to believe.

Shortly after I came to this devastating realization, I attended a Bible study session in which we discussed the effects our thoughts can have on our lifestyles. The preacher said that our thoughts are the foundation of what we come to believe in our minds, which then influence what we believe in our hearts, and then what lies in our hearts eventually presents itself in our speech. Therefore, "I don't know what made me say that" is often a cop-out. We say what we believe to be true.

In my case, I may want to believe that a man walking into my life will make me cry tears of joy. However, in reality, I still believe that men walk out on me and produce the opposite kind of tears. It is difficult to confess, but obviously something that I must admit if I ever intend to change it.

That is what I am doing now: changing my beliefs by rewriting my mental dialogue. I am starting with Faith's song, making a conscious attempt to nail the correct lyrics every time I sing it. I am making a concerted effort to focus on the positive stories I hear about love rather than dwelling on the tales of heartbreak. I am speaking positivity into my thoughts about love and marriage. That optimism has always been there, as evidenced by many of the things that I have written, but it is often overshadowed by negativity. The two competing views have made for some difficult times in my head, but I am determined that in the end, "These three [shall] remain: faith, hope, and love." And "the greatest of these is love." (*1 Corinthians 13:13, NIV*)

Tears of Joy

To date,
Elation has inspired neither poem nor tear.
Rather, a blend
Of adoration, contemplation, and desolation
Have been the source of the most sincere
Words that I have penned.

It is not that I have not known
Happiness or success,
Not that I don't consider myself blessed,
Nor that I have walked
Through each season of life depressed
And bewildered.
My feelings have been stirred
By laughter and delight.
But it is the most extreme emotional states
That inspire me to create—
The moments that shackle and weigh down your heart
Until it drags across your soul's floor,
The situations that open the door
Of your mind
And play ping pong on its walls,
The love that prompts your spirit to crawl
To your heart's altar
And lay prostrate before the Lord—
Those are the emotions
That have implored
Release through word or tear.
But I am still awaiting the moment
When extreme jubilation will make its premiere.
For I wonder if extravagant joy
Produces tears that taste any different on my lips—
Perhaps sweeter?
Or poems with a meter
So allegro
That it causes the poet to stutter,
And a message so exuberant
That it sets the audience's hearts a-flutter?
Surely the difference will be obvious
When the muse is joyous?

Happy tears,
When you grace me
With your presence,
When you finally pool in my eyelids
And spill the emotions of my heart
Upon my face,
I promise to immortalize you
In the form of art.
I will greet you with open arms
When you finally come along,
Not subjecting you
To questions of where you have been
Or what took you so long.
I will not prolong our bonding.
I will wield a pen
And capture all of your corresponding
Emotions
In the only way familiar to me.
Happy tears,
I will honor your coming
And illustrate your beauty
In the words of my poetry.

A Promised Destiny

My life is too precious to leave to chance.
None of this is by happenstance;
Every detail planned before
I was even a thought in my parents' brain.
So I maintain
That every open or closed door
Is a gateway to a future
Written in God's careful penmanship.
In moments of fortune and even hardship,
I know that His hands have a strong grip
On their delicate creation.
He is in full command of every situation's outcome.
So whatever the enemy means for my degradation
Can be turned to fulfill God's purpose.
Every talent and skill
Is an exclusive,
Uniquely designed
To represent His interests and achieve His will.
Every hopeless circumstance is conducive
To a miracle.
Times of confusion in which all earthly evidence is inconclusive
Can be preambles to an oracle
Directly from God's heart to mine.
Every person with whom I've had the delight or distress of crossing paths
Is an accessory to a divine aftermath.
There is purpose in every place to which I have been led,
New life arising from everything I must pronounce dead.
Every word He's ever written or spoken
Is a vow that will never be broken,
A token of His love to carry with me.
And every iteration of His affirmation
Produces a recurring epiphany
That life is but a journey
To a promised destiny.

Run Your Own Race

I took great pride in completing my first 5K. Not being much of a runner, the training process was a real eye-opener. Interestingly, the biggest lessons had applications well beyond running. As you run lap after lap in your life race, here are some things you should keep in mind.

1. It's all mental.

I was talking with a runner friend long before I officially declared my intent to run a 5K. I told her that I just could not seem to run much more than a mile.

"Why do you think that is?" she asked.

Ummm... because that's when I'm too tired to go on?

I do not remember exactly what she said, but when I thought it over later, I had an aha! moment that would make Oprah proud: my one-mile road block was more mental than physical.

In hindsight, I usually told myself that I needed to at least get to a mile. Therefore, when I met that requirement, my mind gave my body permission to quit. However, when my brain declared one mile a midpoint rather than an end point, when I decided that I would not stop no matter how much it hurt, my body surrendered to my thoughts.

Life is no different. It's all mental. If you offer yourself an out, you will take it. If you grant yourself permission to quit, you will do just that. If you are more focused on the pain than on the end goal, you will never make it. But if you can get your mind off the ailments, if you can settle into a stride, if you can focus on the finish line, you will succeed.

2. Run your own race.

During the race, it was nice running alongside other people. There was a sense of camaraderie, with everyone working toward a common goal. After the first hill, I realized I was going to have to walk for a bit. I felt bad about it—until I noticed several other people slow to a walk at that point as well.

Feeling validated in my need to walk, I stopped beating myself up and focused instead on preparing to run again.

We can be really hard on ourselves. We plan to do things a certain way and at a certain time. When we fall short, the disappointment and shame can be paralyzing. However, seeing other people struggle in the same area is oddly encouraging. It reminds you that you are not alone. It assures you that the difficulty you are experiencing is the result of your humanity rather than a personal deficiency.

However, as comforting as it was to know that others also needed to walk after that rough stretch, I soon identified another problem. In following the cues of some of the other runners, I was walking more than I had during my practice runs. I was giving other runners too much influence over me; content just to keep up, I was running beneath my capabilities.

At one point, when I found myself enviously looking at someone who decided to take another walk, I realized that I could not allow myself to walk just because she was walking. For all I knew, she may have been running the last time I walked. In fact, when the going got tough, I had no energy to keep up with what someone else was doing; I needed every ounce of strength to focus on my own race.

So I made up my mind yet again, this time to set my own pace, neither killing myself trying to keep up with hardcore runners nor allowing myself to slack with those who were slower than me. I needed to give my best regardless of what everyone else was doing.

Happy, successful people know the value of setting their own pace in life. It is easy to perform below your abilities simply because that is the level at which everyone else is performing. You may not even realize you are doing it. However, when you stop looking around and instead look internally, you will sense that you have failed to challenge yourself. And that feeling will nag you until you consent to live up to your potential.

But there is another side of the pacing struggle: focusing on those who appear to be running ahead of you and becoming discouraged that you are lagging behind. When you reach a certain age in life, if you are not careful, every birthday will carry angst about where you should be, what you should be doing, and what letters should either precede or follow your name. You will deem yourself a failure or count your life less blessed because you have not attained what others have or what you assumed you would have acquired at this point in the race.

That line of thinking is not only ineffective but counterproductive. As with my run, you need every ounce of your energy to focus on your own life. You can kill yourself trying to keep up with other people or with timelines you developed in middle school. You can forfeit your joy and your gratitude that way as well. Trust that your unique race is being held on the best possible course *for you*. Then ask God for the grace and wisdom to run at your own pace.

As I wrap up the latest leg of my life race by publishing this book, I am both relieved that it's over and thankful for the lessons it taught. I have renewed confidence in myself, greater faith in God, and excitement for the next leg. I am in a good place. This is a good pace.

Notes

1. Dapo Torimiro, Frank Ocean, Midi Mafia. "Quickly." *Evolver*, 2008.
2. James Rowe, "Love Lifted Me," 1912.
3. Civilla D. Martin, "His Eye is on the Sparrow," 1905.
4. *Holy Bible*, NIV, Romans 7:14-25, www.biblegateway.com, 2014.
5. *Holy Bible*, NIV, Jeremiah 29:11, www.biblegateway.com, 2014.
6. *Holy Bible*, King James Version (KJV), Romans 8:28, www.biblegateway.com, 2014.
7. *Holy Bible*, NIV, Psalm 103:12, www.biblegateway.com, 2014.
8. *Holy Bible*, KJV, John 19:30, www.biblegateway.com, 2014.
9. *Holy Bible*, NIV, Hebrews 2:18, www.biblegateway.com, 2014.
10. *Holy Bible*, KJV, Philippians 3:14, www.biblegateway.com, 2014.
11. John Newton, "Amazing Grace," 1779.
12. *Holy Bible*, KJV, Philippians 2:12, www.biblegateway.com, 2014.
13. "Trayvon Martin Shooting Fast Facts," CNN, www.cnn.com, January 28, 2014.
14. Paul Laurence Dunbar, "We Wear the Mask," *Lyrics of Lowly Life*, 1896.
15. India.Arie et al., "Private Party," *Testimony: Volume 1, Life & Relationship*, 2006.
16. *Holy Bible*, NIV Version, 2 Peter 3:8, www.biblegateway.com, 2014.
17. *Holy Bible*, KJV, Romans 5:3-4, www.biblegateway.com, 2014.
18. *Holy Bible*, KJV, Matthew 6:33, www.biblegateway.com, 2014.
19. Edward Mote, "The Solid Rock," *Hymns of Praise*, 1836.
20. *Holy Bible*, KJV, Isaiah 40:31, www.biblegateway.com, 2014.
21. *Holy Bible*, NIV, Matthew 17:20, www.biblegateway.com, 2014.
22. Jean Schwartz, Milton Ager, and Ned Wever, "Trust in Me," *At Last!* 1961.
23. *Holy Bible*, KJV, Haggai 2:9, www.biblegateway.com, 2014.
24. Curtis Jackson, "21 Questions," *Get Rich or Die Tryin'*, 2003.
25. William McDowell, "I Give Myself Away," *As We Worship Live*, 2009.
26. Dwayne Michael Carter, Jr., "How to Love," *Tha Carter IV*, 2011.
27. Herman Colbert Croft and Joyce Croft, "I Can't Even Walk (Without You Holding My Hand)," 1975.
28. "Who is Malala?" *The Malala Fund*, www.malalafund.org, 2014.
29. "Timeline: The Murder of Emmett Till," PBS, www.pbs.org, 2014.
30. Shawn Carter, "Song Cry," *The Blueprint*, 2001.
31. Karyn White, "Superwoman," *Karyn White*, 1988.
32. Beyoncé Knowles et al., "Ego," *I Am... Sasha Fierce*, 2008.
33. Maya Angelou, "Phenomenal Woman," *And Still I Rise*, Random House, 1978.
34. Erica Campbell and Warryn Campbell. "God in Me," *The Sound*, 2008.

35. Hezekiah Walker, "99 ½," *By Any Means Necessary*, 1997.
36. Curtis Burrell, "I Don't Feel No Ways Tired," *I Don't Feel No Ways Tired*, 1990.
37. *Holy Bible*, New KJV, 1 John 4:18, www.biblegateway.com, 2014.
38. Susan Dyer, "Walk with me Lord," 1856.
39. C. Austin Miles, "In the Garden," 1912.
40. *Holy Bible*, NIV, James 1:17, www.biblegateway.com, 2014.
41. *Holy Bible*, New KJV, 2 Corinthians 12:9, www.biblegateway.com, 2014.

29519233R00107

Made in the USA
Charleston, SC
15 May 2014